Praise for *God in the House*

In his role as priest, Tony Kosnik challenged us all to be adult Catholics and form consciences by which we could make sound and Gospel-centered decisions. In his role as educator, he expanded his students' ability to think and to be their best selves. In his role as friend, he made us feel welcome and accepted in his presence.

The late Bishop Thomas J. Gumbleton, written upon Tony Kosnik's death in 2017

I have publicly said that Tony Kosnik was the best pastoral theologian in the Catholic Church in the United States. Thanks to Margaret Stack, we now have a study of Kosnik's work as head of the committee appointed by the Catholic Theological Society of America to produce a contemporary study of human sexuality. Kosnik and his committee denied the existence of absolute norms governing sexuality, but proposed general guidelines based on the values and meaning of human sexuality. The Vatican condemned the Kosnik book. Stack develops the position that this book is an important attempt to understand a Christian approach to human sexuality today. Stack's book is a significant contribution to the search for a contemporary Christian understanding of human sexuality.

Charles Curran, Catholic theologian and retired university professor at Southern Methodist University

Margaret Stack's *God in the House* lovingly describes the remarkable faith-journey of Anthony Kosnik. As widow, friend, and collaborator with the former priest and ethicist, she warmly describes his remarkable life and enriches this inspiring narrative with her expertise as a clinical psychologist.

Suzanne Sattler, IHM, co-author of *No Guilty Bystander: The Extraordinary Life of Bishop Thomas Gumbleton*

God in the House tells the story of the turbulent recent decades of the Catholic Church through the lens of a courageous priest, an accomplished professional woman and the marriage they forged in sync with values that matter most, especially kindness and humor. Author Margaret Stack draws on her own expertise as a clinical psychologist in recounting the life and teaching of her late husband, the Rev. Anthony Kosnik. Kosnik was the theologian whose prophetic scholarship resulted in his banishment from the seminary where he spent 38 years. Documenting how the Catholic Church lost touch with the ethics of sex, Stack writes: "Tony presented sexual ethics in terms of a set of values to be upheld rather than acts to be avoided."

Bill Mitchell, former publisher of *The National Catholic Reporter*

I was privileged to know Tony Kosnik, and I'm delighted that his widow Margaret Stack has so well captured his vigorous intellect, his personal warmth, and his all-embracing love of life. At a time when a rigid orthodoxy threatens to engulf religious practice today, Tony Kosnik's more humanistic approach points to a better way.

John Gallagher, journalist and author of *Rust Belt Reporter: A Memoir*

Vatican II brought with it a significant change in the Catholic Church's understanding of spirituality. For those seeking deeper communion with God, pre-Vatican II spiritual direction had routinely counseled a "flee the world" mentality. Vatican II, in its call for Church engagement in the world, opened us to finding and experiencing God in and through the world, especially in deeper human relationships. And if pre-Vatican II spiritually had fostered a "hierarchical" form of holiness, with celibate priests and nuns at the "top," Vatican II emphasized a "universal call to holiness" rooted in baptism. For many of us, this was a momentous change!

Tony Kosnik played a significant role in helping to bring about this much-needed change in the Church's mindset. In *God in the House*, Peggy Stack has presented Tony's life in all its simplicity and complexity. She both presents the rationale behind his advanced theological understanding of human sexuality and his Christ-like response to all that came into his life, always seeking to respond to others with kindness and concern. For those like myself who are "spiritually inclined," *God in the House* is an inspiring read!

Tom Lumpkin, Detroit priest active in the Catholic Worker Movement

God in the House

The Life and Times of Catholic
Theologian Anthony Kosnik

Margaret Stack,
Ph.D., ABPP

For more information and further discussion, visit:

GodInTheHouse.com

Cover design by Rick Nease
RickNeaseArt.com

Author photo by Rodney Curtis

Published by Read the Spirit Books, an imprint of
Front Edge Publishing
42807 Ford Road, No. 234
Canton, Michigan, 48187, United States

Front Edge Publishing books are available for discount bulk purchases for events, corporate
use and small groups. Special editions, including books with corporate logos, personalized
covers and customized interiors are available for purchase. For more information, contact
Front Edge Publishing at info@FrontEdgePublishing.com.

To our grandchildren, Seb and Vic

"Long may you run."
(Stills-Young Band)

Contents

About the Cover

My sister, Elizabeth Crank, is the visual artist who created the painting for the cover. She wanted to paint a still life, and she asked me to find an object that would be a meaningful symbol of Tony's life. I thought about the many objects in our house that were important to him, including his chalice and paten, the alb that he wore for ordination with the crocheted detail (created by his mother), his wooden statues of the "worried Jesus," numerous crucifixes, and other pieces of artwork from his time in Rome. The most important, however, was in the garage—a bucket with some of Tony's plastering tools. I had given many of Tony's tools to one of his nephews, but I held onto the bucket and a few of the tools. I didn't know why at the time. It was just something that I wasn't ready to let go of.

Plastering was an important and valued skill in Tony's life, and there are many stories about plastering handed down from elders in the Kosnik family. This was a skill that Anastazy, Tony's father, taught his sons. The plaster had to

Author, Margaret Stack, and her sister, Elizabeth Crank.

be mixed with the right proportions of plaster, lime, and water. The rule was that you had to start in the closet until you achieved some mastery of the technique.

As Tony was teaching me about plastering, he would say that I shouldn't worry about making a mistake, that everything could be fixed. I told the story of the plastering and my sister's painting to my spiritual director, Faith Offman, whose comment seems to capture its meaning for Tony.

"There is no unforgiveable sin."

Margaret Stack, Summer 2025

Preface

Margaret "Peggy" Stack and I first met in 1995, when she joined the faculty in the Psychology Department at the University of Detroit Mercy. I had been teaching there for several years, extending my knowledge of developmental psychology into learning more about human sexuality. By the time Peggy joined us, I had been teaching human sexuality to undergrad students, and I was about to assume responsibility for the human sexuality class for the grad students in our clinical psychology Ph.D. program. I needed help, particularly because so many students wanted to sign up for this class in our Catholic university. Peggy was asked to teach an undergrad section of human sexuality, and she did that, with great reviews from the students. The next year, she assisted me in my first crack at working with the grad students. By 1998, with the approval of our chairperson and our dean, we had arranged to co-teach the human sexuality class for the Ph.D. students. Our first team-teaching experience was in 1998, and we taught together until 2021, when we both retired from academia.

At first, I wasn't sure how this collegial relationship would work. The idea seemed to be a good one from a pedagogical viewpoint. The developmental psychologist could approach the material from the viewpoint of normal human behavior, and the clinical psychologist could approach it from the viewpoint of abnormal behavior. But we're talking about human sexuality. For ages, humans have wrestled with what is normal in sexual interactions with others, and in one's own private sexuality. Humans have murdered, and, indeed, continue to murder other humans over these questions. In my own teaching, I had realized that thinking through and discussing these issues with young adults was extremely challenging. And Professor Margaret Stack became an essential intellectual partner for me in gaining some clarity as, with our students, we explored these issues.

It's hard, sometimes, to remember how slow the progress has been, when it comes to understanding sexuality. Or perhaps the national lurching back-and-forth has given us all whiplash. We live in the country where the right to abortion was acknowledged by the Supreme Court (Roe v. Wade) in 1973 and then taken away and left to the various states in 2022 (Dobbs v. Jackson Women's Health Organization). We live in the country where, in 2015, same-sex partners gained equal recognition under the law (Obergefell v. Hodges), but then in 2023 the Supreme Court declared it legal for businesses to discriminate based on sexual orientation (303 Creative v. Elenis). Our national ambivalence and inconsistency about sexual matters has certainly been reflected in decision-making on college campuses, particularly at religiously affiliated schools.

When Peggy and I began teaching human sexuality to students who were hungry for information and the opportunity for safe discussion, it was a time when our first campus gay-straight alliance club communicated by word of mouth, for fear that their meetings would be sabotaged by other students who opposed them. Recognizing that the Catholic archdiocese had forbidden the sale of condoms on campus and teaching about birth and contraception, we would notify our students when the Wayne County Public Health outreach mobile unit would be parked on a nearby off-campus street. We reasoned that half of our students were not Catholic. Why shouldn't they have access to the information and supplies that they needed? It was a constant challenge to balance our students' needs, and principles of academic freedom to explore the truth, with restrictions imposed on us by church hierarchy and the broader culture.

Gradually, I came to know that Peggy had her own life partner, Anthony "Tony" Kosnik. Tony had spent decades wrestling with many of these very issues, first inside the confines of the Catholic Church hierarchy, and then outside the hierarchy but still deeply connected to his Catholic faith. All three of us had been raised to be observant Catholics. For seven years of my young adulthood, I was a Sister of Mercy, and then I left the convent and Catholicism, and I eventually chose Judaism, though I still had great affection for the Sisters of Mercy and felt comfortable teaching at a Catholic university. Peggy describes herself today as a practicing Catholic, who has always been involved in groups promoting Church reform. Those groups included the Detroit Catholic Pastoral

Alliance and Elephants in the Living Room. Like me, Peggy chose to teach at a Catholic university, where she learned more about Ignatian spirituality from the Jesuit priests, and more about social justice from the Sisters of Mercy.

Tony was a priest for forty-seven years before marrying Margaret Stack, who was his intellectual and spiritual partner by then. Tony had remained close to the power centers of the Church hierarchy for a longer time than either of us women had, and his questions and criticisms from inside that power center meant that the Church came down on him with hard and unrelenting judgment. As his closest confidante and partner, Margaret Stack is the perfect person to describe Anthony Kosnik's lifelong struggles with the Church he loved. As she writes in the introduction to this book, "This is an important story about a man who struggled to give voice to his experience in an attempt to contribute to Church teaching on sexuality." This very Church, she adds, was struggling with its own failure to deal with child sexual abuse, misogyny, divisiveness, and "a general disregard for the contributions of the social sciences to our understanding of the human person." These struggles are the storyline for this book, and Tony Kosnik's words of caution and words of objection are documented here, along with the words of other key colleagues and associates who stood up alongside him in the face of the hierarchy.

Over the years, Tony became a regular guest speaker on ethics in our human sexuality class for Ph.D. students. They asked him about the sexual abuse scandal in the Catholic Church, and he talked about that with great honesty and moral clarity. He lectured on ethical decision-making in sexual questions. For many of our students, believe it or not, that was a new way of thinking about sexual interactions, and it was interesting to watch their faces as they confronted that fact about themselves—that they had not thought about sex as an area of personal ethical decision-making. Over many years, I have learned that human sexuality classes should be taught in person, so that teachers and students get used to reading one another's faces as they speak about sex. This cannot happen when all the faces, including your own, are in tiny squares on your personal computer screen, or your cell phone.

Margaret Stack's book documents how Tony Kosnik's thinking about sexual issues changed over the years, heavily influenced by what he heard as a priest, hearing the confessions of Catholics tortured by guilt over using birth control, considering divorce, engaging in "deliberate" masturbation, and pursuing same-sex intimacy. Tony's lectures and writing revealed how he had come to regard the whole person, in context, as the focus of this ethical decision-making regarding sexual issues. In Tony's thinking, everything became a "question of values for healthy relationships," Peggy writes in the chapter documenting Tony's 1977 publication on *Human Sexuality*, a study that he compiled with other experts and theologians. She also describes how the Church dealt with Tony and his colleagues, to attempt to control them and punish them afterwards. That part of the story is disappointing, but equally fascinating and important.

As Margaret Stack's book goes to press, Pope Leo XIV has been elevated to lead the Catholic Church globally. Questions abound: Will he be welcoming to members of LGBTQ+ communities? Will he close the door, or will he summon them to the Church, as did his predecessor? What will this American/Peruvian Pope say about abortion? Birth control? Divorce? How much autonomy will Pope Leo XIV grant to various cultural communities in terms of urging them to rely on their own consciences, as Tony put it?

Anthony Kosnik's voice was not a voice in the wilderness, or a voice to be forgotten. We still need his voice—and we can hear him clearly in this memoir.

Carol Cronin Weisfeld was born in Chicago, and obtained her doctorate in Human Development from the University of Chicago in 1980. That year she began teaching at Mercy College of Detroit, which merged with University of Detroit in 1990. She taught Human Development, Health Psychology, and Human Sexuality at the University of Detroit Mercy until retirement in 2018. Together with her husband, Glenn Weisfeld, and their many students and colleagues across the globe, she studied and wrote about the lives of married couples for forty years. With her husband, she still lives in her adopted city of Detroit.

Introduction

This is a story about my husband, the Reverend Anthony Kosnik, who was a Catholic priest of the Archdiocese of Detroit, ordained in 1955. He co-authored a book, *Human Sexuality: New Directions in American Catholic Thought*, sponsored by the Catholic Theological Society of America and published in 1977, that challenged traditional Church teaching on sexuality. The focal point for Tony's conflict with the institution has been Church teaching on sexuality. This story centers on that conflict, although it is a much bigger story.

Tony was raised in a large and traditional Polish Catholic family in Detroit. He was formed by his experience of family and his experience of Church. This is a story about his formation and transformation within a relational, cultural, and religious context, that is, familial, Polish, and Catholic.

This is an important story about a man who struggled to give voice to his experience in an attempt to contribute to Church teaching on sexuality. And it is a story about an institution that has continued to struggle to rise above the damage to its credibility related to the uncovering of longstanding sex abuse by members of the clergy, misogyny reflected in its treatment of women, divisiveness that has come out of the Second Vatican Council of the 1960s, and a general disregard for contributions of the social sciences to our understanding of the human person.

My perspective in writing this story is as Tony's wife, but also as a social scientist, a clinical psychologist. My perspective provides a framework for telling his story. I first met Tony when I was completing my Ph.D. in clinical psychology in 1982. This was a moment of crisis in his life, related to the publication of *Human Sexuality*. He had been fired from his job at the Polish seminary in Orchard Lake, Michigan, and he was in the process of finding a new direction for his work. In 1983, he began teaching at Marygrove College in Detroit, where he directed the pastoral ministry program. He also taught at Ecumenical Theological Seminary, where he directed their doctoral program for a time. At the same time, he was involved in many other endeavors, including ethics consultation and participation in groups that worked on reform of the Church (e.g. Call to Action, Elephants in the Living Room, Catholic Council) and political reform (e.g. Catholics for the Common Good). Over the years, we also collaborated in teaching and various workshops on human sexuality, in which we attempted to integrate our (respective) theological and psychological perspectives. This collaboration has certainly informed my work. Although I am left to tell the story alone, I hope that his words and his work will come through clearly.

Through my teaching and my clinical work, I have come to understand that for each of us, there is a movement toward wholeness. This has been characterized by different social scientists as a movement toward "self-actualization" (Maslow, 1970), the fully functioning person (Rogers, 1961), generativity and integrity (Erickson, 1963). William James (1902) talks about qualities of "saintliness." In theological terms, this movement might be described as redemption, conversion, a "quest for the living God" (Johnson, 2007). Christian fundamentalist groups talk about being "saved." We are somehow moved to come out of ourselves, to reach beyond the confines of fear, indecision, others' expectations, to be more, to make meaningful contact with others (with God?), which propels us to the next period of growth. When we are thwarted in this movement, the consequences may take the form of physical infirmity, unhappiness, problems with adjustment, mental illness, narcissism, acting out in destructive ways. Some individuals manage to persevere through the roadblocks to their development to realize their potential. I believe that Tony's story reflects this kind of perseverance.

Institutions may also be said to engage in a movement toward wholeness. Systems theory (Haley, 1987; Minuchin, 1974; Bowen, 1961 and others) provides a useful framework for understanding and intervening with social groups, such as families, work groups, and larger institutions. A system is a defined group that includes its members and their interactions with each other. According to this theory, systems work to achieve their stated purpose, with a strong pull toward maintaining integrity and staying together. We can see this dynamic in small groups, such as the family. In institutions such as the Catholic Church, we can see attempts to preserve and protect basic values and belief systems related to their stated purpose. Institutional churches across a variety of denominations tend to be more conservative, as their focus is on protecting and preserving basic values.

The individual and the system are interrelated. The interactions of individuals within a system have been described as a kind of intricate folk dance (Minuchin, 1974). The members know the steps and know their part. When someone tries a new step, it throws off the other dancers. This may be perceived as a threat to the integrity of the group and to its stated purpose. In its attempt to protect integrity and core values, the system may retreat into dysfunction. A system may be viewed as dysfunctional when its efforts to maintain integrity and to preserve basic values involve setting rigid boundaries that restrict the work and contributions of individuals, poor communication, problems with resolution of conflict, shutting down of strong feelings, and isolation. The effects on members of such groups are harmful. It is very hard to live and work and/or grow up in such a system.

Institutions are hard on those who are "out of step," and may attempt to silence, ostracize, or sanction such individuals in other ways. The prophets of our time, such as Bishop Gumbleton, Rev. Oscar Romero, and Dorothy Day, have certainly been perceived as "out of step," and have had to deal with the institutional response to their movements. Maybe it is consoling to think of oneself as part of this kind of group. As Tony worked to rise above his own struggles with the institution, it was clear that he loved his Church and saw himself as one with God's holy people.

Left: Tony and I dancing at a family wedding in 2007.

Right: This picture captures Tony's response to new life, wherever he found it. He is standing with a recently planted tree in front of the house on Doremus in Hamtramck—looking heavenward. I call this stance a "movement toward wholeness."

Last Words

It makes sense to begin this story with its ending. Anthony Raymond Kosnik died at 8:30 p.m. on September 22, 2017. It was the last day of Rosh Hashanah. Although I didn't realize it at the time, it was also the birthday of Tony's closest friend, Stasiu. Tony and Stasiu entered the high school seminary together. Stasiu always sat in the seat behind him (Kosnik, Kukulski ...), cracked jokes, got him into trouble more than once or twice. Tony and Stasiu were ordained together. They talked and argued and prayed and played golf and traveled together over the years. Eventually they established an email correspondence. Tony would print Stasiu's daily missives, which later filled many boxes. Stasiu died in 2005, shortly after the fiftieth anniversary of their ordination. In the months before his own death, Tony would ask about him.

In the two years before his death, Tony struggled with multiple health issues, problems with mobility, and dementia. The dementia came gradually. I believe that he noticed

long before any of us did. Tony was very good at holding it
together and probably held the dementia at bay in its early
stages. I have a new appreciation for the concept of neural
networks, connections, pathways. Tony established lots of
networks, had many friends. As any good theologian will
do, he reflected on his experience, all of his experience. I
commented later to my friends that this would have been
interesting if he wasn't my husband. At times, it was heart-
breaking to watch. I can remember him standing in the
hallway sometime in 2015, telling me that he felt alone and
isolated. This was not the Tony that I knew. The computer
didn't work. His cell phone was useless. And he could no
longer turn on the TV.

I have tried to go back and piece together a chronology
of the things that he said (and did) during this last period.
Statements, moments that stood out. As I attempt to do this,
to enter his experience, he reminds me that my thoughts are
not his thoughts. So I will try to stick to the script, stay with
his words. But these fragments do connect back to a larger
story.

I was looking through Tony's documents on the computer
and came across a letter that he wrote on April 4, 2015, to
the leadership of a group called Catholics for the Common
Good. After he left active ministry, Tony continued to work
for reform in the Church, and for political reform. To these
ends he had been active in two groups, the Elephants in the
Living Room and Catholics for the Common Good. The
latter group had been holding meetings in our home because
it was hard for Tony to get out. *My abilities are fading faster
than imagined, and I just wanted to make sure everything is
handed over. It has been a great privilege and blessing working*

with all of you. Tony could no longer give workshops, lead marches against injustice, or write letters to the archbishop. But he didn't want the work to stop, and didn't want to let anyone down. He always said, *Thank you.* To the end, he would thank me for each task that I performed for him.

Together we also joined Regroup, a support group for priests and women religious who had left active ministry to get married. During this time, Tony's participation in Regroup changed from giving support to being fed and cared for. Beginning in August 2016, members of Regroup organized "Tuesdays with Tony." They took turns staying with him on Tuesday afternoons when I had to teach. On one occasion, our friend, Paula, had come to stay with him. Tony asked, *Are you the lifeguard?* To which she replied, "Yes, and I know how to swim." They both had a good laugh. Paula reported another conversation. Tony said to her, *When you get up in the morning, you probably know who you are, where you are, and what day it is. I don't. It takes me a long time.* Our friends brought conversation, encouragement, emotional support, and dinner to these visits.

Throughout that year, there were little signs. In March, he sent an email to his friend, Ron Modras, one of the co-authors of *Human Sexuality*. Ron had sent an article for him to read. *I would like to read it. All is well. This could be my last effort.* I sent him for bagels one morning, and he couldn't find the bagel store. He went to pick up our granddaughter from a school activity a mile from our house and struggled to find his way home. In October 2016, I had to go out of town for work. I left on a Tuesday afternoon and came back Wednesday evening. Tony's sister Angie came to stay with him. On Wednesday morning, she heard him calling, *I need help.* He was struggling to get out of bed and was trying to keep himself from falling. This was also an acknowledgment of a deeper understanding of his condition and marked the beginning of rapid and significant decline.

We started hospice in March 2017. He seemed to welcome this change. The hospice nurse came weekly. I reviewed the notes in his patient chart. I would report "more confusion" at these visits, and he would report *no pain.* On June 24, 2017, we traveled to Suttons Bay for our annual family vacation, which also included my son, his partner, and our two grandchildren. Shortly after we arrived, Tony took me aside and said, *I need to talk to you privately.* He announced that he expected to die that night. *Who will administer the last rites?*

After that week, he wanted to be home, whenever we, or he, were not. *I want to go home. I'm ready to go home. Please take me home.* And, *Where is my wife?* whenever I would leave. I would always explain carefully where I was going and when I expected to be back. If it was more than an hour, he would forget and would search for me frantically. Finally, in August 2017 he told me, *My mother said that I can't be left alone anymore.* Our close friend and pastor, Paul Chateau, came and administered the last rites.

On the last day of August 2017, he asked Marilyn, one of his caregivers, *Can you tell me who I am and what's going on?* He was trying to pull together the disconnected thoughts, images, and memories, but he couldn't do it this time. Two weeks later, I left home briefly to run an errand. Somehow he was able to make the cell phone work. *Margaret, I am lost.*

There were some still shots: Tony holding three-month-old Matthew Bryce on June 21, 2017, his eighty-seventh birthday. Happy. Content. Observing the wedding of his niece, Diana on September 2, 2017. Observing, not presiding. Squeezing my hand as the couple recited their vows. Holding Matthew again at his baptism on September 17. Happy. Content. And the last series of still shots. I made his favorite steak dinner on September 22. He enjoyed the meal, had ice cream for dessert. I left the room briefly and came back to find him clearing the table. Tony died as I was helping him to bed. He struggled for interminable minutes and then let out a loud groan. Silence.

Top: Tony with Matthew Bryce, September 17, 2017. This was taken at a family party for Matthew after his baptism, five days before Tony's death.

Bottom: Members of Regroup with Rev. Paul Chateau at a gathering in 2015.
Left, to right, front to back:
Row 1: Tony Kosnik, Dave Zaffina, Ed Haggerty, George VanAntwerp
Row 2: Peg Stack, Paula Zimmer, Mary Haggerty, Pat Harrington-Hooper, Rev. Paul Chateau, Mary Lou VanAntwerp
Row 3: Aileen Cronin, Glenn Jollimore, Patty Feighan, John Harrington-Hooper
Row 4: Norman Brault, Colleen Brault, Dave Britz, Peg Britz
Row 5: George Cronin, Bob Livingston, Mary Sue Livingston, Bob Schaden, Judy Janes

2

In the Beginning

*You know me through and through, from having watched
my bones take shape when I was being formed in
secret, knitted together in the limbo of the womb.*

(Ps. 139, 15)

The task I have undertaken is to pull together pieces collected from Tony's life to provide some understanding of
how he was formed, in and through his family, his relationships, his formal and informal educational experiences, and
his church. These are not so separate. How did he come to
be the person he was? How did he come to think the way he
did and, finally, to say what he had to say?

What are the pieces? Family stories, pictures, letters sent
and received, my memories of our lived experience, mine
and others' recollections of things he said, diplomas and
certificates, Tony's writings (including his doctoral dissertation, articles, a book chapter, *Human Sexuality*), class notes,
lectures, homilies, a family history compiled by Tony's
niece, Michelle (Molz, 2002), newspaper clippings, trip logs,
journals, more pictures, emails from his best friend Stasiu,
invitations sent and received, his First Communion prayer
book, the collection of tools in our basement—including

trowels and plastering stuff, pipe wrenches in every size, and projectors—in every closet and storage space.

Maybe the bigger question is, how to put it all together? What is really important? And how do I know? I remind myself to stick to the script, let his story tell itself. Listen. Stay out of the way. My years of clinical training and experience have prepared me well for this last task that I will perform for him.

Anthony 'Tony' Raymond Kosnik was the sixth of thirteen children born to Anastazy and Angeline (Gorzenski) Kosnik. In the end, there were ten boys and three girls. The first nine children were boys. Tony was born at home, 17928 Norwood, in Detroit, Michigan, on Sunday, June 21, 1930. The family story is that his mother reminded him more than once over the years that he made her miss Mass that day. (Angeline was a daily communicant.) Anastazy and Angeline were second generation Polish Americans, who moved to Detroit from Bay City several years before Tony was born. It is not clear whether English or Polish was the first language in the home. His First Communion prayer book was in Polish. Tony later learned many languages and was fluent in five or six.

The family identified as Polish, American, and Catholic. They were active in Corpus Christi parish, 18045 McDougal, Detroit. The parish, which opened in 1923, was closed in 1989 and is now home to a Protestant congregation. Corpus Christi was identified as a Polish ethnic parish. In 1985, half of the parishioners were of Polish descent. Corpus Christi is translated as "body of Christ," and it is celebrated each year in late spring as a feast in the Catholic church, honoring what is believed to be the real presence of Jesus in the Eucharist. In

Europe, there are grand celebrations with colorful and long processions—one of which we witnessed during a trip to Poland in 2005. It went on for miles, no repeats.

For Tony's family, religious feasts and observances marked the seasons: Advent, Christmas, Lent, Easter. One's "name day" was celebrated on the day of the year corresponding to the feast of the saint who had the same given name. It was like a birthday. Tony's saint was Anthony of Padua, and his name day was June 13. Sacraments marked developmental passages: Baptism, new life; Penance, Eucharist, Confirmation, coming of age; Matrimony, Holy Orders, adult commitments; and Extreme Unction (Last Rites, Sacrament of the Sick), transition to death. Formal prayers, such as the Mass and the Rosary, marked the days and weeks. Except for the day of Tony's birth, Angeline attended Mass every day, and she gathered her children to say the Rosary each evening. In 2009, Tony suffered a cardiac arrest and was hospitalized for a month. His brother, Bernie, came every day and recited the Rosary with us. At the end, Tony held onto his rosary, and I left it with him when he was cremated. It seemed wrong, somehow, to take it then.

We have a beautiful carved wooden plate hanging in our living room. It is from Poland, and the saying on the plate can be translated as "A guest in the house is God in the house." The saying follows from a very strongly held religious belief in the real presence of Jesus in the Eucharist (Corpus Christi). In the Kosnik household, there was always room for a guest at the table and an extra bed for anyone who needed to stay—grandparents, travelers, students, relatives, relatives of relatives, friends of relatives of relatives. Lots of people. Sharing the oplatek (angel bread) at Christmastime was another important way that this message was conveyed. The oplatek wafer, like a communion wafer, is seen as a reminder of God's presence. Much like the Jewish Yom Kippur, "day of atonement," the sharing of the oplatek is a gesture of reconciliation and peace.

Anastazy Kosnik built the house on Norwood, adding rooms later that were needed for his growing family. He told his sons that they could do anything they wanted to do. This was not to promote a disregard for the rules, but rather to (strongly) encourage study and hard work. Anastazy worked the first shift as a metal finisher at the Chrysler plant on Detroit's east side. He would come home in the afternoon, have dinner, and then put his sons to work in the construction and renovation business that he operated on the side. Tony and his brothers learned carpentry, plumbing, masonry, painting, plastering, and electrical work. One of the rules during this training was that you started plastering in the closet, so that your early mistakes would be hidden. Tony's brother, Bernie, tells the story of being assigned to do the tile work on a construction project, with the expectation that he would teach himself how to do it. (Throughout his life, Bernie did wonderful tile work.) All of the brothers learned the construction trade, and all obtained advanced degrees so that they wouldn't have to earn their living this way. Although, they certainly valued their early experience and put it to good use. The Kosnik brothers remodeled a home on Doremus in Hamtramck for their parents in 1965—after the children were grown. And they remodeled it again for Tony so that he would have a place to live after being fired from the seminary in 1982. The house on Norwood is still standing, still well-kept.

One of the stories that Tony liked to tell was the story of his first mortal sin. At some point during his teenage years, he was asked by his father to work on a construction project at a Baptist church. He had to choose between loyalty to his father and loyalty to his Catholic upbringing, which taught at that time that it was a sin to enter another church. Tony chose to obey his father. He would laugh when he told the story, but it was an important moment.

Still later, after we had been married a few years, Tony and I walked through an older house purchased by my niece, Sarah, and her then fiancé, Derek, just before they were married. It was a house built in 1928 and remodeled in the 70s with shag carpet and holes punched in the plaster walls of the living room to make room for shelves. Sarah and Derek had searched far and wide for someone to repair the plaster and restore the old house—with no success. As we were leaving, Tony said, *We could do that.* And "we" (the groom, the mother of the bride, various members of the wedding party, and myself, under supervision of the bride) did. Tony showed us how to mix the plaster and repair the walls, matching the texture that was there. We finished two days before the wedding. The best outcome of this project for Tony was that Derek later mixed up some plaster on his own and repaired the wall next to the basement stairs.

The gender roles in the 1930s were more traditional, although Angeline insisted that all of her children learn to grow and can fruits and vegetables, bake, cook, keep house, and crochet. There exists a beautiful tablecloth, crocheted by the brothers, that has since been appropriated by Tony's nephew, Tom. And when the girls insisted that they be included in the construction work, they were taken on a job.

Tony described his father as firm and demanding, fair and loving. In talking about his mother to his niece, Michelle, as she was compiling the family history, he said: *She drove the family car from the earliest days, long before other women drove. She loved to travel, see things, go anywhere. She loved life and communicated that with all her being.* Angeline also had a sense of humor. She told her children that she "should have entered the convent" when they were out of line.

There were other lessons. Tony's earliest memory was from an incident that occurred when he was about six years old. He remembers going with his mother and some of his siblings to the Chrysler plant, where Anastazy was participating in a strike. They brought him a lunch, which they had to throw over the fence. Based on the timing of Tony's recollection, Anastazy would have been taking part in the Chrysler sit-down strike of 1937, perhaps the largest strike in U.S. history. This was an important moment in the U.S. labor movement. On March 8, 1937, workers at Dodge Main began what was to be a seventeen-day sit-down strike to gain Chrysler's recognition of the U.A.W. Workers stayed in the plant for the duration of the strike, which ended on March 25, 1937. Chrysler recognized the U.A.W. on April 7.

It is clear that Tony took his father's examples to heart—both mixing plaster for the Baptist church and taking part in the Chrysler strike. Throughout his priestly ministry, he would encourage people to form and to follow their well-formed conscience—above all else.

The notion of family, and the value placed on family, were also deeply engrained. Family means that you belong, no matter what. Everyone is welcome. It means that you have each other's back, that you love and respect each other, that you take care of each other, that you work and play (hard) together. And it means that you are not afraid to call each other out when something isn't right. Being family is a generative experience, always creating something new. The bonds are not formed lightly, and these intimate points of connection were characterized by Tony's family of origin as "God in the house." Tony would sometimes quote Shakespeare on this point: "Those friends thou hast, and their adoption tried, grapple them unto thy soul with hoops of steel" (*Hamlet*, Act 3). The Book of Ruth says it in different words: "Wherever you go, I will go. Wherever you live, I will live. Your people shall be my people, and your God, my God" (Rt. I: 16).

Snapshot of Tony's family, early 1940s. Left to right:
Back row: Bernie, Ed, John, Joe, Anastazy, Leonard
Middle row: Frankie, Tony, Angeline holding Dorothy, Patrick
Front row: Annie, Paul, Ted, Angie (in front of Leonard)

Kosnik family celebrating the fiftieth wedding anniversary of Angeline and Anastazy. Back row, left to right: Leonard, Ed, Joe, John, Bernie, Tony, Frankie, Patrick, Paul, Ted Front row, left to right: Dorothy, Annie, Anastazy, Angeline, Angie

REGISTRATION CARD—(Men born on or after February 17, 1897 and on or before December 31, 1921)

SERIAL NUMBER	1. NAME (Print)			ORDER NUMBER
T 2158	ANASTAZY (First)	LESTER (Middle)	KOSNIK (Last)	T 11,980

2. PLACE OF RESIDENCE (Print)

17928 NORWOOD DETROIT WAYNE Mich
(Number and street) (Town, township, village, or city) (County) (State)

[THE PLACE OF RESIDENCE GIVEN ON THE LINE ABOVE WILL DETERMINE LOCAL BOARD JURISDICTION; LINE 2 OF REGISTRATION CERTIFICATE WILL BE IDENTICAL]

3. MAILING ADDRESS

Same

(Mailing address if other than place indicated on line 2. If same insert word same)

4. TELEPHONE	5. AGE IN YEARS	6. PLACE OF BIRTH
none	44	BAY CITY (Town or county)
(Exchange) (Number)	DATE OF BIRTH MAY 1 1897 (Mo.) (Day) (Yr.)	MICH (State or country)

7. NAME AND ADDRESS OF PERSON WHO WILL ALWAYS KNOW YOUR ADDRESS

ANGELINE KOSNIK

8. EMPLOYER'S NAME AND ADDRESS

Chrysler Corp KERCHEVAL PLANT

9. PLACE OF EMPLOYMENT OR BUSINESS

KERCHEVAL DETROIT WAYNE Mich
(Number and street or R. F. D. number) (Town) (County) (State)

I AFFIRM THAT I HAVE VERIFIED ABOVE ANSWERS AND THAT THEY ARE TRUE.

Anastazy Lester Kosnik

D. S. S. Form 1 (Revised 1-1-42) (over) ☆ GPO 16—21630-2 (Registrant's signature)

Left: 3308 Doremus, Hamtramck, rear view. Right: front view.

Bottom: Anastazy Kosnik WWII draft card, 1941.

Church of Corpus Christi

McDougall at Nevada

RECTORY—18080 Mitchell . . . Telephone: TWinbrook 2-0332
CONVENT—18010 Mitchell . . . Telephone: TWinbrook 2-4552
SCHOOL—18045 McDougall . . . Telephone: TWinbrook 2-3120

MASSES: Sundays 7 (Polish), 8, 9, 10 (Polish), 11:30, 12:30
Holydays: 5:30, 7, 8, 9, 10, 11:30 and 7:30 p.m.
Daily: 7, 8

CONFESSIONS:
Saturday; day before First Friday and Holyday: 3:30—5:00; 7—8:00
Instruction—Public School Children, Wednesday at 4:00

BAPTISMS:
Sunday at 2 p.m. Parents must make arrangements
beforehand at rectory.

REV. MITCHELL J. WITKOWSKI, Pastor

REV. STANLEY C. KUKULSKI

REV. A. SZYMANOWSKI

Corpus Christi Parish bulletin 1955, year of Tony's ordination.

Top: Tony's parents, Anastazy and Angeline Kosnik, early 1920s.

Bottom: Tony plastering third floor at Doremus in Hamtramck, 1980s.

3

Indelible Mark

You are a priest forever, according to the order of Melchizedek.
(Ps 110:4)

*There are eunuchs born that way from their mother's womb,
there are eunuchs made so by men and there are eunuchs
who have made themselves that way for the sake of the
kingdom of heaven. Let anyone accept this who can.*
(Matt 19:12)

Tony left home at age thirteen to attend the high school
seminary, St. Mary's Preparatory School at Orchard Lake. St.
Mary's was a boarding school located on the campus of St.
Mary's College and Sts. Cyril & Methodius (Polish) seminary. This move was encouraged and apparently facilitated by
his eighth-grade teacher, Sister Doloretta, from the Corpus
Christi parish grade school, which he attended. While the
rule was that "only students who express[ed] a sincere desire
to explore their interest in the priesthood should be invited
to join high school seminary programs," Tony admitted that
the opportunity to (finally) have his own bed was a strong
motivating factor in his decision to accept admission and
scholarship to this program. Later, as he began his undergraduate studies at St. Mary's College, he would embrace the
ideals of the Catholic priesthood, including chastity, purity
of heart, and dedication to a life of leadership and service.

Tony received his B.A. from St. Mary's College in 1951 and began his formal studies for the priesthood at St. John's Provincial Seminary in Plymouth, Michigan, the same year. He was twenty-one years old.

From a developmental perspective, thirteen-year-old boys are beginning a process of significant change in weight and stature, sexual functioning, and brain growth, precipitated by hormonal changes. This is a time of idealism, of questions about identity, authority, and relationships, and a time of learning to manage emerging strong feelings and impulses with an adolescent brain. During adolescence, the brain is developing processes involved in direction and control of thinking and behavior, that is, executive functions, which depend on the maturation of the frontal lobes during late adolescence. For Tony, the context for all of this change was the all-male high school seminary environment. This was a structured environment that provided clear rules for behavior and promoted internalization of a strong moral code. His days were marked by daily Eucharist and classes in theology—in addition to the high school curriculum, regular participation in the sacrament of penance and spiritual direction, and devotional prayer. Polish culture was valued and promoted at St. Mary's. All of this likely provided important connections to Tony's early family life. He had left home, but the terrain was familiar.

Tony developed a strong interest in moral theology, and he eventually received his Doctorate in Sacred Theology (S.T.D.) from the Angelicum University in Rome, with a major in moral theology. His doctoral degree was posted in June 1960. The date is important. Prior to 1960, training in this area emphasized the use of "manuals of moral theology"

(Curran, 2008, p. 63), which focused on the question: "What actions are wrong or sinful in light of Catholic teaching?" (p. 63). This model posited absolute norms for behavior, based on an understanding of natural law (i.e. what is our nature as human beings?) as "being universal, absolute, and unchangeable" (p. 63). In judging right and wrong, the emphasis was on the act rather than on the person and context of the act. This set the tone for his studies in moral theology, beginning in the high school seminary. Tony's doctoral dissertation, *The imputability of acts of masturbation among males* (1951), perhaps provides a glimpse of his early efforts to reconcile an aspect of his sexual experience with his theological training.

In the high school seminary, Tony was surrounded by other adolescent boys considering the diocesan priesthood as a life path. He thus acquired a new family, and he began to develop a close relationship with his new brother, Stasiu, which would endure for life. Girls, the focus of Tony's affection and attraction, however, were conspicuously absent from this picture. Home visits were limited to one weekend a month. Tony did go on a few dates, but there were no important romances during this period in his life. The life he was preparing for involved a commitment to celibate chastity, which meant forgoing marriage and other sexual relationships.

Tony was ordained to the priesthood on June 4, 1955, by Edward Cardinal Mooney, at Blessed Sacrament Cathedral in Detroit. He celebrated his first Mass the next day, June 5, at his home parish, Corpus Christi. He was twenty-four years old. Tony put together an album of photographs from the ordination and his first Mass. The format is that of a

wedding album, beginning with a copy of the announcement of his ordination and invitation to his first Solemn
Mass and first priestly Blessing and Benediction—a copy in
English and another copy in Polish. These are followed by
a series of elaborate black and white photos of these events,
including robing for the ceremony, flowers, pictures with
his mother and father, pictures with his family, and a long
procession to the parish church with banners. One that I
recognize is of Our Lady of Czestochowa and a group of
nieces and a nephew in their white First Communion attire.
The photographs of the ordination captured the important
components of the ceremony, and for each part there is a
small faded typed explanation inserted with the larger picture: Prostration and the Litany of the Saints, Bestowal of
the Office, Anointing of the Hands, Communion of the
Ordained, Bestowal of the Power to Forgive Sins, and the
Unfolding of the Chasuble. During this "unfolding," the
bishop says, "May the Lord clothe thee with the robe of
innocence."

What were Tony's thoughts as he lay prostrate on the
floor of the sanctuary? For the sake of what kingdom did
he make this commitment? What did he feel as the bishop
and priests silently presented imposed hands, marking the
moment of "transformation [taking] place in the soul of the
ordinand, which makes him 'Priest forever according to the
order of Melchisedek'"? What is the indelible mark on his
soul? It is important to note that this mark is believed to
endure forever, regardless of individual choices, even if he
were to leave active ministry. I have searched my own experience for a referent to understand this. What comes to mind
is my experience of holding and calming my son shortly after

his birth. I remember the moment of silent commitment to accept the responsibility of caring for him always. For me, this has been an "indelible mark."

We have friends, Pat and Fred, whose marriage Tony witnessed in 2003. Fred was a diocesan priest who left active ministry after thirty-five years to marry Pat, a retired teacher and divorced woman with several adult children. On the occasion of Fred's fiftieth anniversary of ordination, June 2018, Pat honored Fred with a "Melchizedek Celebration" to observe his fifty years of ordination as a priest. Fred explained that Melchizedek, for whom the bible provided no information about parentage or death, represents "a priesthood that is unique and eternal." The celebration, which included family members and many close friends, was joyful. During the event, Mass was celebrated by their pastor. Dancing was encouraged.

Tony later served as Professor of Ethics and Moral Theology at St. Mary's College and Sts. Cyril & Methodius Seminary (1961 to 1983), where he had begun his own studies. Toward the end of his tenure, in 1982, he was abducted at gunpoint by two youths from Pontiac, ages fifteen and seventeen. This incident occurred on Saturday, March 13, 1982. Tony had gone to the drug store at Square Lake Road and Woodward and was approached by the youths. They apparently thought he was a wealthy businessman. They took him in (I think) his car and drove around—one of the youths pointed a gun at him. After driving around for some time, they decided to stop at a bank so that he could take out money for them. When the car slowed, Tony managed to kick the door open, and he ran to a nearby restaurant for help. What was memorable to Tony about the incident was not that he could have been killed. (He seemed to have retained some sense of invincibility.) While he was being driven around in his car at gunpoint, he was asked where he lived and what he did. Tony tried to explain to these youths, who had no point of reference for his experience, what a seminary was and what a priest did there. He had trouble with the explanation.

Top: Tony as a young priest.

Bottom: Kosnik family, June 5, 1955, on the occasion of Tony's first Mass.
Left to right: Paul, Frankie, Ted, Leonard, Anastazy, Ed, Tony, John,
Angeline, Annie, Dorothy, Patrick, Angie, Bernie, Joe.

Top: Photo taken at Tony's ordination on June 4, 1955.

Bottom: Tony's first mass, June 5, 1955.

PONTIFICIUM ATHENAEUM INTERNATIONALE « ANGELICUM »

Rev. ANTHONY R. KOSNIK

THE IMPUTABILITY OF ACTS
OF MASTURBATION AMONG MALES

DISSERTATIO

AD LAUREAM

IN FACULTATE SACRAE THEOLOGIAE

APUD PONTIFICIUM ATHENAEUM « ANGELICUM »

DE URBE

ROMAE

1 9 6 1

Front cover of Tony's dissertation, 1961.

Revisiting Angelicum University, Rome 2008.

Tony at Orchard Lake seminary.

4

Vatican II

I want to throw open the windows of the Church, so that we can see out and the people can see in.

Attributed to Pope John XXIII, speaking about Vatican II, quoted by R. DeRoo.

*Another version: "Throw **open the windows** of the church and let the fresh air of the spirit blow through."*

This chapter has been hard to write. The opening to this material for me was a dream that I had several weeks ago, just after Easter. I had a "big" dream, described by Jung (1989) as a dream marked by archetypal imagery, thought to tap into ancient and universal themes and symbols, such as death and rebirth and the hero. I dreamed that Tony was found to be alive, that he hadn't really died. He was in a bed, and we were in a big room, like a dormitory or a hotel room. The room was crowded with people who had been close friends of Tony during his lifetime. They were planning to stay. One of these friends, a woman religious, told me that Tony needed a nurse. (I remembered that she was not a nurse.) I was frantically searching for his transport chair and for items of clothing that I thought he needed. I found the chair, but only the top part of the chair, handles and back. I never found the clothing, although I searched in our house, in all of the places I could think of where I might have put his things away. At some point during the dream, not at the end,

I was lifting Tony up. He was very light, and I think he was wearing a white garment. I woke up wondering how to get all of these people out of our room.

The dream speaks of Easter themes of death and resurrection, the empty tomb, the white garment, as well as being weighed down by the cares of the world. I found the images to be both vivid and distressing for some time. This lasted until I began to think about where the dream was leading. Jung's view of dreams is teleological, pointing to the future. Being able to lift Tony up, to forget about the chair and the clothes, seemed more significant in this light. Maybe telling his story is lifting him up somehow, opening the window, defying death. Or the dream is not only my dream.

Tony studied in Rome from 1958 to 1961. He completed his Doctorate in Sacred Theology (S.T.D.) at the Dominican Angelicum University in Rome in 1960. He received his degree in Canon Law (J.C.B.) from the Gregorian University in Rome in 1961. During this period, Tony lived at the Polish Institute, Via Pietro Cavallini 38. Each day he walked across one of the bridges over the Tiber to the Angelicum, where he studied moral theology. He told me that he liked to buy a bunch of grapes from a fruit vendor and eat them while he walked. We traveled to Rome in 2008 and we took this walk together, beginning at the Polish Institute, crossing over the bridge, and then approaching the Angelicum and exploring its library. We didn't have grapes, but we managed to find a $20 cup of coffee at an outdoor cafe.

Being sent to study in Rome meant that Tony was being prepared to become a bishop, the Catholic Church's version of "the brightest and best." This did not happen for a variety of reasons, but it appears to have been the original intent of his superiors. Studying in Rome during this period was also important because it meant that Tony was in Rome at the time of the election and installation of Pope John XXIII, October 28, 1958. He was there when Pope John XXIII announced his intent to summon a council (January 25, 1959), and during the years of preparation for Vatican II, which was formally opened on October 11, 1962.

Vatican II was the twenty-first Vatican council, called by Pope John XXIII and completed under Pope Paul VI. There had been only twenty-one Ecumenical Councils called over a period of approximately 1,600 years. Vatican II was directed at a detailed examination of doctrine, life, and worship in order to "bring ... the modern world into contact with the vivifying and perennial energies of the gospel, a world which exalts itself with its conquests in the technical and scientific fields, but which brings also the consequences of a temporal order which some have wished to reorganize excluding God" (*Humanae Salutis*, John XXIII, December 25, 1961). The historical context for this event was a world "on the brink of destruction," due to widespread poverty, injustice, and fears about nuclear war. In its process, this council represented a shift from doctrine and hierarchy to dialogue. "More than anyone else, [John XXIII] transformed the dominant symbol of the Vatican from that of a pyramid, with vertical lines of authority, seeking to impart wisdom unilaterally, to that of a circle, with all members equal in dignity and in capacity to serve" (R. DeRoo, 2012, p. 14).

Vatican II was a "big" event, both with regard to its magnitude and its significance. There were more than 2,500 bishops from many different parts of the world who participated in this event for a four-year period. The bishops were assisted by more than one hundred scholars with doctorates in their respective disciplines. The council included a group of observers from other churches or faiths. Although this group did not speak directly during the council proceedings, their private conversations with the participants had an impact. For example, they were able to make constructive suggestions, which were passed on to commission leaders. DeRoo maintains that the media and women also had an impact, although women were "not on the agenda."

Out of this process came a new understanding of the People of God, which included the laity and the notion of "servant leadership" of ministers; a "new compassionate relationship with the world;" conscience formation and social justice teaching—with a "preferential option for the cause of the poor;"—liturgical renewal; expansion of ideas about "real presence" of God; and ecumenism and interfaith dialogue. Vatican II formally asked the question, "Church, who are you?" And the image of the Church as a "pilgrim people," called to give service in the light of "Gospel values" emerged. Both ministers and lay persons were viewed as having an important role, and the "basic baptismal vocation of all believers" (DeRoo, p. 70) was recognized. Leadership in the Church was to be founded on service rather than power. This council acknowledged solidarity with the world and the struggles of all people to make meaning, to survive, and to ensure the survival of all. Teaching on social justice was emphasized, including a commitment to the poor and marginalized, and an avoidance of war as a means of solving conflict. Conscience formation in this context was seen as a matter of personal responsibility, leading to a response to social issues. Liturgical renewal meant using meaningful language, such as in the celebration of the Eucharist. And the "real presence" of Jesus referred not only to the sacred host, but to multiple manifestations of "presence," such as in the sacraments, Scripture, the person of the minister, and the entire congregation praying and singing. Ecumenism and interfaith dialogue meant recognizing that all were partners in the search for truth. Overall, there was an emphasis on basic values, rather than doctrine, and an understanding of faith as a relationship with God.

Tony was twenty-eight years old and beginning his graduate studies at the time of the election and installation of Pope John XXIII. He was profoundly affected by this event and by Vatican II, which shaped his thinking and his theology. In retrospect, it must have appealed to his very deep sense of what was right and true. This began with his earliest experiences of family, and his father as a role model, particularly in his actions plastering the Baptist church and participating in the Chrysler sit-down strike of 1937. Throughout his life, Tony's value of the family and the sacred quality of these relationships was most basic and important for him. So, the "window" that opened for him at the time of Vatican II allowed light to come in and light to go out. At some level, Tony recognized these new ideas as connected with his early life, and this marked the beginning of the transformation of his thinking.

In his understanding of moral theology, Tony moved from the "moral manuals" to a deeper understanding of values, context, and relationship. As he lectured in this area, he talked about the "well-formed conscience," or developing the capacity for moral reasoning through reflection on Scripture, experience, and Church teaching. The application of this was to act, not out of allegiance to an abstract doctrine, but out of one's own deeply held convictions, to be able to live with oneself. Tony spent much of his academic career teaching people to serve as ministers in the Church, beginning with the training of men for the priesthood at Sts. Cyril and Methodius Seminary in Orchard Lake (1961 to 1983). Later, he trained lay persons, including women and people from other faith traditions, to serve as ministers. He directed the Pastoral Ministry program at Marygrove College (1983 to 2000) and served as a member of the faculty at the Ecumenical Theological Seminary during this same period.

Moving out of the seminary in 1983 opened another window for Tony in that he began to live on his own. He began to develop relationships with his neighbors, friends, and family in a different way. He celebrated the Eucharist with his friends in their homes, or in his home, as well as in the parishes where he helped out on weekends. On Holy Thursday, he would gather his friends for Mass and dinner at his home, rather than attend the special Mass held at the cathedral for priests of the archdiocese. In June 2005, on the fiftieth anniversary of Tony's ordination, we had a dinner in our home for the men from his ordination class and their wives (if they had left to marry). Tony got some plywood and constructed a round tabletop for our dining room table so that we could sit in a circle. It allowed for a very different kind of conversation, with everyone participating.

Over the last forty-plus years, there has been much disparaging of Vatican II by more conservative elements in the Catholic Church. There is an attempt to return to the "moral manuals" and a re-translation of liturgy. The "new" liturgy is marked by archaic language and sentence structure, as well as an implicit dualism, of the body and soul. This represents an attempt to close a window that really can't be closed. I think it was like this for Tony. Once he started thinking, he couldn't go back.

Top: Tony at the installation of Pope John XXIII, Rome 1961,
seated next to a woman wearing a white mantilla.

Bottom: Tony with his Sistine Chapel umbrella.

Top: This was taken during Tony's studies in Rome.
Charles Curran and Tom Hinsberg are also seated at the table.

Bottom: This is the round table that Tony constructed for the
celebration of his fiftieth anniversary of ordination.

5

Human Sexuality

*Human Sexuality: New Directions in American Catholic
Thought: A Study Commissioned by the Catholic Theological
Society of America. New York: Paulist Press, 1977*

*Sexuality is the Creator's ingenious way of calling people
constantly out of themselves into relationship with others.*

(Kosnik, et al, p. 85)

In an interview about family history with his niece, Michelle,
Tony recounted his first lesson in sexuality. The lesson was
provided by his cousin Theda, who told him that "the lady
[he] was calling 'fat' was really pregnant and proceeded to
explain in great detail all that that meant" (Molz, 2002, p.
28). He was nine years old. His mother had a stroke after giving birth to Angeline in July 1939. Tony and several siblings
had been sent to spend the rest of that summer with their
Aunt Martha and Uncle Ray and assorted cousins, including
Theda, who lived in a trailer on the farm of Uncle Leo and
Aunt Jenny in Flushing, Michigan.

Tony attributed his first lessons in love, however, to his
early experiences with his parents and family. Whenever he
would preach at a marriage ceremony, he would talk about
"the school of love" provided by the couple's respective families. While this may not always have been true for the couples
whose weddings he witnessed, it was true of the Gorzenski/

Kosnik family. Tony's own parents were warm and loving with each other, with their children, and with members of their extended families. This part of his family culture has persisted. Leaving a Kosnik family gathering takes a long time because you hug everybody as you leave. These are not perfunctory hugs. These hugs say: You belong. You matter. I care about what happens to you. When I married Tony, his brother, Bernie, told me that I was not just marrying Tony, but I was also marrying the family. They have continued to regard this as a solemn commitment.

In the fall of 1972, the Board of Directors of the Catholic Theological Society of America (CTSA) established a committee to do a study on human sexuality. "The circumstances which occasioned the study can only be described as a massive breakdown of Catholic adherence to traditional Church teachings on sexuality" (from a press statement, CTSA Committee on Human Sexuality, May 25, 1977). The specifics of this "breakdown" included: rejection of the Church's teaching on birth control by a majority of U.S. Catholics and a majority of Catholic priests, acceptance of premarital intercourse for engaged couples, and questions about the sinfulness of "deliberate adolescent masturbation." An important task of the committee, as described by the CTSA Board of Directors, was to "provide some helpful and illuminating guidelines in the present confusion." The final report of the committee was published as a book by Paulist Press in 1977.

The committee included Rev. Anthony Kosnik (later named chairperson), priest of the archdiocese of Detroit and professor of moral theology and dean at Sts. Cyril and Methodius Seminary, Orchard Lake, Michigan; William

Carroll, certified psychologist and trial lawyer, and professor of law at the John Marshall School of Law in Chicago, Illinois; Sister Agnes Cunningham, member of the Servants of the Holy Heart of Mary, associate professor of patrology and Church history at St. Mary of the Lake Seminary, Mundelein, Illinois, and vice president of the CTSA Board of Directors; Rev. Ronald Modras, priest of the archdiocese of Detroit and associate professor of systematic theology at St. John's Seminary, Plymouth, Michigan; and Rev. James Schulte, director of instruction at the St. Joseph's Hospital School of Nursing in Marshfield, Wisconsin.

The academic credentials and experience base of the committee members were extensive. According to William Carroll, their selection was guided by their areas of expertise, as well as by "other practical concerns" (personal communication, May 2019). The latter included concerns about "not unnecessarily provoking an immediate alarm on the part of episcopal authority." For example, Tony was well-regarded by other moral theologians, and he was professor and dean of a "solidly safe and conservative" seminary. In addition, consultation on the work of the committee was provided by twenty-five theologians.

The process for preparing the CTSA report was important. This was not the work of one individual but rather represented collaboration among the members of the committee, the coauthors of the final report. The process was described to me by William Carroll (personal communication, May 2019). The initial meeting of the group was directed at understanding the parameters of the task and scope of the undertaking and also involved some discussion of possible "unspoken assumptions" held by members of the committee. A chairperson of the group was not formally selected, although Tony took the lead in managing the work of the committee and was eventually named as chair. "Tony always seemed to be the one who took the lead in arranging the practical matters of our exchanging tentative drafts, determining time and locations for meetings, running off notes taken at recent meetings. Eventually he was the one that others contacted to learn how things were progressing and to make their suggestions as to what should be addressed in our work. Tony never 'shouldered' his way into this leadership position. His quiet awareness of things that had to be done and his willingness to do the 'grunt' work without any show endeared him to us all." The work itself was divided based on the variety of interests and relative levels of competence among the coauthors with regard to the issues to be addressed by the study. Over the period of 1972 to 1976, members of the committee "exchanged papers on the various subjects and then met ... to exchange views, critique, and sharpen our focus. At these meetings, members would bring along relevant ideas and writings of other theologians and members of the CTSA they had come across, or specific issues members of the society wished addressed." All commented on the outside suggestions and concerns.

In the preface to the final report, the coauthors noted that "this study is not a collection of separate essays authored by different members of this committee. Although individual members may have prepared initial drafts and contributed more to certain sections because of their particular expertise, the entire work was discussed, modified, reviewed in detail, and approved by the committee as a whole. Our rules for procedure allowed for the inclusion of dissenting or minority positions. Much to our surprise and satisfaction, however, the mutual openness and sharing that prevailed throughout our collaboration resulted in a final product that was acceptable to every member of the committee without substantial disagreement or objection." The theologians who had provided "constructive recommendations" were acknowledged: Gregory Baum, Charles Curran, John Dedek, Dennis Doherty, Margaret Farley RSM, Eugene Fisher, John Glaser, A. Regina Hall, George Kanoti, Mrs. H. June Kuczynski, RN, Richard McCormick, SJ, Giles Milhaven, Timothy O'Connell, Michael Prieur, and Cornelius J. van der Poel CSSp. Editing of the manuscript was done by Sr. Irene Doman.

The "present confusion" which led to the need for this study was reflected in Tony's writings and presentations during the period from 1969 to 1976, prior to publication of the final report. In 1969, he prepared booklets for the Institute for Continuing Education, Archdiocese of Detroit, on *Penance* and *Crisis in Conscience*. He published an article on "Pastoral care of those involved in canonically invalid marriages" (Jurist, 1971). He also wrote a series of articles for *The Michigan Catholic* on morality in 1973, and another series of articles on divorce and remarriage in 1974. He wrote another article on "Forming the Christian Catholic conscience," published in *Hospital Progress*, August 1975. During this period, Tony spoke to various groups: university students, parish groups, seminarians, priests, individuals preparing for ministry, women religious. His lecture topics included: Marriage Theology, Morality, Formation of a Christian Conscience, Divorce and Remarriage, Human Sexuality, Counseling the Homosexual, Did God Want Us to be Sexed? Personhood and Sexuality, Moral and Ethical Aspects of Human Sexuality and Celibacy, The Celibate in the Church Today, and Theology of Human Sexuality.

The 1976 Call to Action Conference (sponsored by the National Council of Catholic Bishops) echoed Tony's responses above to the "present confusion" in its call for "dialogue within the Catholic community on matters concerning human sexuality and a corporate reflection on human experience and gospel values, as well as on Christian tradition and Church teaching. Such dialogue, coupled with serious interdisciplinary research, should provide a means of developing more adequate pastoral care and should assist all persons in the Church to inform their consciences more fully on the moral dimensions of human sexuality" (Origins, November 4, 1976).

When Tony talked about this period (prior to the publication of *Human Sexuality*), he noted that he had been troubled when hearing confessions of individuals struggling with concerns about using birth control, marital problems leading to divorce, and various "sexual sins," including masturbation, premarital sex, and same-sex behaviors. The moral manuals were inadequate as he attempted to respond to the concerns expressed by Catholics who were trying to reconcile their lived experience with Church teaching. While he did not share his responses to penitents directly, his writings and lectures certainly reflected a shift in his thinking, which appears to have led to a more pastoral response. Another glimpse of this was provided by people who came to Tony's wake and funeral, many of whom wrote to me to say that his pastoral response had been important for them and/or their families.

The final report of the CTSA committee included material on the Bible and human sexuality, Christian tradition
and human sexuality, and the empirical sciences and human
sexuality as foundational "for good pastoral theology and
practice." From this foundation a theology of human sexuality and pastoral guidelines for human sexuality were
developed. *Human Sexuality: New Directions in American
Catholic Thought* represents a "personalist" perspective on
human sexuality. This perspective considers what it means
to be a human person and attempts to look at the whole
human person, in context (Janssens, 1990). The procreative dimension of sexuality (emphasized in formal Church
teaching over the centuries) is presented as one aspect of the
total reality. It suggests a broadening of the traditional formulation of the purpose of sexuality "from *procreative and
unitive* to *creative and integrative*" (p. 86). The question of
the morality of sexual behavior is framed as a question of
values for healthy relationships, i.e. presumed to foster creativity and integration. Sexual behavior that is "conducive to
creative growth and integration of the human person," must
be "self-liberating, other-enriching, honest, faithful, socially
responsible, life-serving, and joyous" (pp. 92-95).

Tony was forced to leave his teaching position at Sts. Cyril
and Methodius Seminary in 1982 because of his work on
Human Sexuality. In a letter to Bishop John Quinn, President
of the National Conference of Catholic Bishops, from a representative of the Congregation for the Doctrine of the Faith
(which represents the teaching authority of the Catholic
church), the official response of the Church was made clear:
"... the Congregation cannot fail to note its concern that a
distinguished society of Catholic Theologians would have

arranged for the publication of this report in such a way as to give broad distribution to the erroneous principles and conclusions of this book and in this way provide a source of confusion among the people of God" (Franjo Cardinal Seper, Congregatio Pro Doctrina Fidei, July 13, 1979).

I have a short video clip of Tony at our granddaughter's First Communion on June 7, 2015. It was taken by one of my sisters and shows Tony from the back, standing with me, participating in the liturgy. He is eighty-four years old and thirteen years into our marriage. You can see the back of his neck, his new haircut, and the back of his green tweed suit coat. (And tie, which you can't see, but imagine, because he is wearing it.) His stance is prayerful, focused, reflective, and utterly respectful. It provides a glimpse of his relationship with his Church, as well as with his God. Solid. Faithful.

Widely published news photo of Tony with three of the co-writers of Human Sexuality: (left to right) James Schulte, Tony, William Carroll, sister Agnes Cunningham.

With Ron Modras (co-author of *Human Sexuality*)
and his wife Liz Hogan, Madrid, 2008.
Left to right: Liz Hogan, Tony, Peggy, Ron Modras.

Kosnik,
et al.

HUMAN SEXUALITY

HUMAN SEXUALITY

New Directions in American Catholic Thought

A Study Commissioned by
The Catholic Theological Society
of America

PAULIST
PRESS

Original book cover for *Human Sexuality*, Kosnik et al.

6

Aftermath

Weeping may endure for the night, but joy comes in the morning.
(Ps. 30, v. 5)

Those friends thou hast, and their adoption tried,
grapple them unto thy soul with hoops of steel.
(Hamlet, Act 3, Wm. Shakespeare)

For Tony, the outcome of his involvement in writing *Human Sexuality* unfolded over a period of six years. The publication date was May 1977. The report was submitted to CTSA on June 10, 1977. And the official release date for the book was June 20, 1977. In the meantime, it had been submitted to the Sacred Congregation for the Doctrine of the Faith, which represents the teaching authority of the Catholic Church, as well as to the National Conference of Catholic Bishops. The NCCB issued a "Statement of the Committee on Doctrine Concerning *Human Sexuality*" to the American bishops on November 15, 1977. The Sacred Congregation responded on July 13, 1979.

The Committee on Doctrine (NCCB) noted that it "does not object to a theological study of sexuality offered as a stimulus for discussion among theologians and other qualified people. But it rejects the idea that a tentative study such as *Human Sexuality* can offer 'helpful pastoral guidelines to beleaguered pastors, priests, counselors, and teachers' as well as guidance for the faithful in forming their consciences when such a study contradicts theological tradition and the Church's clear magisterial teaching refined over the centuries and recently reaffirmed in the Vatican Declaration of Sexual Ethics and the American Bishops' Pastoral Letter" (p. 2). The Committee took issue with the critical exegesis of Scripture described in the report, as well as the use of social scientific research. The values presented as guidelines in *Human Sexuality*, i.e. self-liberating, other-enriching, honest, joyous, and faithful, were described as "second level values" which "offer little guidance" (p. 4). The Committee reasserted the Church's position that "the unitive and pro-creative dimension of human sexual activity as it came from the hands of God can be properly realized only within the marriage covenant" (p. 2). The document did note, "We understand and appreciate the need for compassion in dealing with human nature, weakened as it is by sin and subject to strong cultural pressures, particularly in the area of sexual morality" (p. 5). Concern was expressed, however, that pastoral compassion could lead to "weakening the demands of sound morality" (p. 6). It should be noted that Archbishop Joseph L. Bernadine, (then) president of the NCCB, made a statement in his farewell address to this group urging the bishops to establish closer relations with theologians and scholars in order to "help to avoid some of the crises and confrontations" that have arisen over doctrinal matters, such as the controversy over *Human Sexuality*.

The Sacred Congregation sent their response to The Most Reverend John R. Quinn, Archbishop of San Francisco, President of the NCCB. It was forwarded to John Cardinal Dearden, Archbishop of Detroit (Tony's superior),

OBSERVATIONS of the Congregation for the Doctrine of the Faith on the book *Human Sexuality*. In the cover letter to this statement, Franjo Cardinal Seper, Cardinal Prefect for the Sacred Congregation for the Doctrine of the Faith noted, "At the same time, the Congregation cannot fail to note its concern that a distinguished society of Catholic Theologians would have arranged for the publication of this report in such a way as to give broad distribution to the erroneous principles and conclusions of this book and in this way provide a source of confusion among the people of God." The document itself was directed at calling attention "to errors contained in the book," and invited its authors to correct these errors. The Sacred Congregation, first of all, took issue with the definition of sexuality presented in *Human Sexuality*: "Sex is seen as a force that permeates, influences, and affects every act of a person's being at every moment of existence. It is not operative in one restricted area of life, but is rather at the core and center of our total life-response. As the recent Vatican *Declaration on Sexual Ethics* maintains, 'It is from sex that the human person receives the characteristics which, on the biological, psychological, and spiritual levels, make that person a man or a woman, and thereby largely condition his or her progress towards maturity and insertion into society'" (Kosnik et al., 1977, p. 81). OBSERVATIONS countered, "It is not, however, in this area of generic sexuality that the moral problem of chastity is engaged. This occurs rather within the more specific field of sexual being and behavior called genital sexuality, which, while existing within the field of generic sexuality, has its specific rules corresponding to its proper structure and finality."

In line with traditional Church teaching, emphasis is placed on the "primordial importance of procreation." *Human Sexuality* tried to explore and elaborate on the "meaning and value of conjugal love," i.e. the unitive dimension of sexual relating. The Sacred Congregation had difficulty with the statement that "procreation is only one possible form of creativity, but not essential to sexuality" (Kosnik, 1977, p. 83). "This change of purpose and consequently of the criteria for morality in human sexuality evidently changes all the traditional conclusions about sexual behavior." OBSERVATIONS described the values presented in *Human Sexuality* as "determined by personal sentiment," and "purely subjective." They also expressed concern about moral relativism: "The subjection of theological and scientific arguments to evaluation primarily derived from one's present experience of what is human or less than human gives rise to a relativism in human conduct which recognized no absolute values."

On August 16, 1979, Archbishop Dearden wrote to Tony, enclosing with his letter the text of the response from the Sacred Congregation: "In view of the fact that your name is explicitly referred to in the text of the OBSERVATIONS, it seems to me that a response to the Sacred Congregation is called for. I am confident that you will make it with an awareness of the implications of this action by the Holy See. Whatever comments you may wish to make may be made directly to the Sacred Congregation or sent through the office of the Apostolic Delegate. If you take this step, I hope that you will send me a copy of your letter." Evidently, Tony and the archbishop met and discussed this in September 1979. Dearden wrote another letter to Tony on January 9,

1980, inquiring about his response: "In any case, after these many months having heard nothing further about the matter, I do think it reasonable to pursue it with you. I do this on my own initiative, but I am anxious to know what the state of the matter is. I hope that at your convenience you will inform me."

Tony responded to Archbishop Dearden on January 12, 1980:

> *Dear Cardinal Dearden,*
>
> *I received your letter of January 9 inquiring about my response to the Holy See regarding Human Sexuality. I am grateful for your patience in this matter and hope you will understand the reason for so long a delay. The fact of the matter is that I have written not one but many responses. Unfortunately, after allowing several days for reflection and consultation with others, more experienced than myself in these matters, none of them seemed appropriate.*
>
> *The events of the past few months, both personally and in the life of the Church, have not been particularly encouraging and conducive for responding to the Holy See. It is not that I have considered it unimportant. If anything, my friends assure me that I am exaggerating the importance of this response. In any case, after many drafts and much reflection and consultation, I have finally prepared a response that I plan to forward to the Sacred Congregation through the Apostolic Delegate this coming Wednesday, January 15.*

I am enclosing a copy of the response to Cardinal Seper as well as my request to the Apostolic Delegate. Trusting that the response is appropriate, I remain

Cordially yours in Christ,

Rev. Anthony R. Kosnik

SS. Cyril and Methodius Seminary

Orchard Lake, Michigan 48033

This letter provides a glimpse of Tony's discouragement with the controversy about *Human Sexuality* and concern about making a good and comprehensive response to the Holy See. The exchange of letters between Tony and Cardinal Dearden also gives some insight regarding their relationship, which is respectful and collegial.

In his letter to the Sacred Congregation, Tony reiterated the context of the *Human Sexuality* report, commissioned by the CTSA: "The purpose of the study was to bring some theological light and healing to this situation," the situation being "the widespread gap that existed between the Church's official teaching and the manner in which the majority of Catholics were reaching decisions on matters of human sexuality." He noted: "It was and remains my conviction that a good part of the confusion and misunderstanding (about *Human Sexuality*) resulted from the failure to distinguish between the moral ideal or principle proclaimed by the Church and the personal, concrete decision reached by the individual conscience." He defended the use of specific values to be considered in making moral judgments about sexual behavior: "Our own pastoral experience has led us to believe that by raising questions suggested by these values we help persons become conscious and aware of subtle ways of violating sexual integrity and morality that otherwise would never have come to mind. Again, it is also our conviction that far more individual lives have been shattered, far more marriages weakened and destroyed and far greater harm done to society by the disregard for this personal relational aspect of sexuality than by violations of the physical, genital order." In his letter, Tony addressed again the "diverse ways in which this (sexual) relationship is understood." Tony emphasized pastoral concerns, or "questions that must be raised in addressing sexual behavior in the concrete individual person where it is generally acknowledged that the moral principle cannot always be the concrete moral dictate." Finally, he talked about his overriding concern about formation of conscience. "Only when the faithful are able to internalize their convictions and respond from a truly informed and morally responsible conscience is our task as moral educators complete."

The tone of his letter to the Sacred Congregation is tactful, conciliatory, and represents an attempt to continue the dialogue about his work. Tony's response is, however, subtly confrontational on a number of levels. First of all, he is responding directly to the Holy See, and not through his bishop. This is a challenge to the hierarchical structure of the Church and to the prescribed relationships among the faithful. This is evident, for example, in the path of the Sacred Congregation's OBSERVATIONS, from the Sacred Congregation to Apostolic Delegate to the NCCB to John Dearden to Tony. Secondly, Tony is challenging the "moral manuals" (described by Curran, 2008). He questions the use of what he terms "act morality," i.e. judging the individual act rather than the meaning and context of the act. Tony is also raising questions about Church authority when he suggests that it is the well-formed individual conscience that must have the last word about individual choices and behavior.

Tony was granted a sabbatical from May 1980 to May 1981. He celebrated his twenty-fifth anniversary of ordination in June 1980 and then traveled extensively in Poland, where he did research on family history. During the 1981-82 academic year, it appears that the controversy surrounding the publication of *Human Sexuality* had not died down, and was in fact negatively affecting Sts. Cyril and Methodius Seminary. On March 20, 1982, Tony submitted a letter of resignation from the faculty of Sts. Cyril and Methodius Seminary effective July 1, 1982, to Rev. Stanley Milewski, Chancellor of the Orchard Lake Schools. He also sent a letter to then Archbishop Edmund Szoka: *In accordance with your wishes, I have submitted my letter of resignation from the faculty of SS. Cyril and Methodius Seminary to Father Stanley Milewski effective as of July 1st. A copy of the same is enclosed. Since my theology is not acceptable within this Archdiocese, I ask Your Excellency for permission and support in seeking placement in another diocese.* The issue was that Tony had not "undertaken that sort of serious re-evaluation of the committee's conclusions which would ideally have led to a public correction of those points singled out as not in conformity with the teaching and practice of the Church" (letter fragment dated April 26, 1982, author unknown).

The students at the seminary engaged in a formal and organized protest of Tony's forced resignation. Letters of support poured in from other priests, members of religious communities, individuals from various educational institutions, and individual Catholics. Tony saved all of these letters in a very large notebook. My last count was several hundred letters, some directed to Tony, some to Szoka and/ or Milewski. Several other full-time faculty members at the seminary resigned in protest. Efforts were made to arrange a meeting between Tony and Archbishop Szoka, but Szoka was hospitalized with chest pains, so this meeting did not take place. Tony was reinstated, however, on April 30, 1982, just prior to the seminary graduation ceremony—at which a formal protest had been planned.

It happened that I first met Tony during this very difficult period in his life. He baptized my eight-year-old son in February 1982. When my son was an infant, I had attempted to arrange for him to be baptized by the priest who had celebrated my marriage. When I called to make this request, the priest informed me that he could not baptize my son because he was leaving active ministry to get married. I didn't do anything more about this at the time, although I did send my son to a Catholic grade school when it was time. So he learned about the Catholic faith and about the sacraments, and he asked to be baptized when he was in the second grade. I first went to the pastor of my mother's parish, who wanted to treat him as an adult convert. I was uncomfortable with this approach. At that time, I was finishing my doctoral training. One of my clinical supervisors was a psychologist who was also a woman religious (nun). She put me in touch with Tony. He was very respectful and responsive to my request and immediately made arrangements to baptize my son at the parish of the school which he was attending. He met with me and my son together and talked with us about what we were undertaking. It was a very welcoming experience. I had no idea that Tony was in the middle of such a crisis.

In any case, the crisis continued for Tony during the 1982-83 academic year. Among Tony's papers, there is a letter from then Joseph Cardinal Ratzinger (later to become Pope Benedict XVI) to Archbishop Szoka, dated February 16, 1983: "In our meeting on October 15, 1982, I believe we agreed that you would arrange to meet with Rev. Anthony Koznick, who presently teaches on the faculty of the Orchard Lake Seminary in your Archdiocese. It remains the decision of this Congregation that Fr. Koznick must rectify the positions he took in opposition to the clear teaching of the Church in the CTSA study on sexuality. We would be grateful now, if you would let us know how your meeting went, and specifically what Fr. Koznick intends to do regarding his dissenting positions. In addition, we would appreciate knowing what Fr. Koznick's future plans are after his current contract at Orchard Lake is not renewed, if such information is presently available." During this academic year, Tony was interviewing for other positions. He began a position as Director of the Pastoral Ministry program at Marygrove College in Detroit in August 1983.

What did all of this mean for Tony? He certainly experienced betrayal by his friend and colleague, Father Milewski, by his superior, Archbishop Szoka, and (implicitly) by his Church. The apparent disregard for the spelling of Tony's name in the above letter from Ratzinger seems telling. Life as he knew it was turned upside down. Tony moved from the seminary, which had been his home for most of the forty-year period from 1943 to 1983, to the home in Hamtramck (3308 Doremus) where his parents had been living prior to their deaths several years prior. Tony had spent two years at St. John's seminary prior to his ordination, and three years studying in Rome after that. But he had not really lived on his own outside of a seminary context. He would often note later that he was thankful to Szoka for his release from the seminary environment, but this move was quite a transition.

Tony experienced a cardiac arrest on July 6, 2009. We had gone to the gym early that morning, and he collapsed while working out. Tony was attended to immediately. The facility had a defibrillator, and personnel trained to use it. He spent a month in the hospital, on a ventilator for at least ten days, and eventually moved to a step-down unit and then to rehab in the hospital. (If you lie in bed for several weeks, your muscles stop working.) He lived another eight years, but he was very sick at this time. I made the decision not to allow visitors, except for myself and two of his brothers. I was afraid that the stress associated with the number of visitors and their emotional responses to him would result in his death. Only one person managed to get through the security measures that I had set up: then Monsignor Stanley Milewski, Chancellor of Orchard Lake Schools. I had met Msgr. Milewski on several occasions over the years. He was a flamboyant character, bigger than life, the center of attention in his presentation. I had left the hospital for a brief period one afternoon and came back to find a small glass statue of Our Lady of Orchard Lake on the table next to Tony's bed. Tony was still on life support, so he couldn't tell me where it came from. Milewski had let my brother-in-law, Len, know that he had been there. I restrained my impulse to throttle both of them. In retrospect, I think that Milewski thought Tony was going to die, and he came to make amends. I imagine him sitting in the chair in the corner of the room, quietly praying. I hope this is true.

teachers quit to protest priest's resignation

nolics published a contro-
ial book on human sexual-
resigned under pressure
n the school's chancellor,
Rev. Stanley Milewski.

ister Annelise Sinnot, O.P.,
r Josephine Gaugier, O.P.,
Sister Trinita Schelling,
submitted their resigna-
effective July 1, accord-
o Father Koper.

SOURCE close to the situ-
said Father Milewski was
pted to seek Father Kos-
resignation by the Most

Rev. Edmund C. Szoka, archbishop of Detroit.

Another source, an archdi-
ocesan priest who asked not to
be identified, said, "It is clear
that (Archbishop) Szoka wants
to remove (from the archdiocese) any offense to the conservative element of the church.
He listens closely to what
Rome says, and Rome is saying
that the sort of thing Tony
(Father Kosnik) is writing is
just not acceptable."

"And (Father) Milewski
wants nothing more than to
please the archbishop," the
priest said.

The archbishop was out of
town Wednesday and unavail-
able for comment. However,
the Rev. Patrick Halfpenny, a
spokesman for the archbishop,
said the prelate is not engaged
in a purge of liberals. "That . . .
is very obviously an interpretation of the situation, and it's
not an accurate interpretation," Father Halfpenny said."

About 100 seminary stu-
dents and alumni have formed
a "Committee to Reinstate Father Kosnik," according to
Beverly Sinke, an alumna of St.
Mary's college, which is on the
same campus as the seminary.

"We have sent a letter to
Father Milewski asking that he
not accept the resignation. He
must realize that the academic
atmosphere of a seminary that
is preparing men to be priests
in the real world has to go
across a continuum of thought.
The conservatives need to be
heard, so do the liberals. There
needs to be dialogue."

A SPOKESWOMAN for Fa-
ther Milewski said he would
not speak to reporters.

Father Kosnik's resignation
came within several weeks after a seminary evaluation com-

mittee grilled him about his
part in writing the book. The
book questioned traditional
Catholic teachings on sex, saying that there was no Biblical
prohibition of masturbation,
that few Catholics took seriously the church's rules against
pre-marital sex and that the
church should minister pasto-
rally to homosexuals, not condemn them.

Vatican officials invited Father Kosnik and his co-authors
to "correct the errors" in their
book three years ago.

Father Kosnik was unavail-
able for comment Wednesday.

Controversial priest n theological board

The Rev. Anthony Kosnik, who is being
rced by Detroit Archbishop Edmund
:oka to resign his theological professorship
Sts. Cyril and Methodius Seminary in
-chard Lake at the end of the 1983 summer
rm, was recently elected by unanimous
-te to the board of directors of the Catholic
eological Society of America. Father Kos-
c became *persona non grata* with the
atholic hierarchy several years ago when
raised questions about the validity of
aditional Catholic doctrine on sexuality.
e society is the most prestigious gathering
theologians in North America.

WAS IN SEX-TEACHING FLAP
Priest will leave seminary

A priest who has been under fire for his
views on sexuality will leave St. Mary's seminary at Orchard Lake to teach non-theological
courses at Detroit's Marygrove College, sources
said Sunday.

The Rev. Anthony Kosnik, 53, could not be
reached for comment Sunday, but several area
clergy confirmed his transfer. Officials at the
Oakland County seminary could not be reached
Sunday either.

Father Kosnik was co-author of an explor-
atory book published in 1977 that raised questions about official church teaching on sexual
matters, including homosexuality, birth control
and masturbation.

Ever since, there has been pressure from the
Vatican and bishops around the country who
send seminarians to Orchard Lake for Father
Kosnik's ouster.

Despite Father Kosnik's explanation that the
book was commissioned by the Catholic Theological Society of America and did not challenge
church law, but only inquired about its application, he was asked to resign from the seminary
last year.

Only a threatened boycott of the seminary's
graduation exercises by prominent Detroit area
Catholics, including Msgr. Clement Kern, made
seminary officials back down, and Father Kosnik was allowed to remain on the faculty until he
could find another teaching job.

---

op, right: News coverage following Tony's ouster from Orchard Lake, *Detroit Free Press*, 1983.

Left: Announcement of Tony's appointment to the CTSA
Board of Directors. *Detroit Free Press*, June 1983.

Top: On the occasion of Tony's twenty-fifth anniversary of ordination, 1980.

Bottom: Tony at Marygrove College, 1980s.

7

The Company You Keep

Tell me what company you keep, and I will tell you what you are.
Miguel de Cervantes, Don Quixote

For the fiftieth anniversary of his ordination, June 4, 2005, Tony and I held a dinner at our home, inviting all of the members of his ordination class whom we could find. There were thirteen places at the table. The party included one active priest, one widow, one widower, and four other priests with their wives. Tony had gone out and bought two large pieces of plywood, which he cut into half circles and hinged together to make a round top—and then positioned it on top of our dining room table. The round table affected our conversation at the dinner, in that it included all of us at the table. From my perspective, that changed the conversation. We were a company of equals, and we took part in one conversation. Images of the round table and sharing a meal represented significant elements in Tony's approach to ministry throughout his life.

The one still-active priest who accepted our invitation to dinner, Rev. Norm Thomas, had ministered for many years in a large parish in the city of Detroit. Norm was not known for following protocol. Someone at the table asked him how he came to be who he was, outspoken, a champion for the underserved and underrepresented in our city. He laughed, looked around the table, and said, "It's the company I keep."

The ordination class of 1955 at St. John's Seminary in Plymouth, Michigan included a number of very dedicated and active priests who went on to minister in Detroit. *The Detroit News* published an article on December 17, 1993: "Seminary's bad boys of '55 are now among city leaders," highlighting the accomplishments of some of these men, whom they termed "hell-raisers ... now Detroit's heavy hitters." This group included Tony, Rev. William Cunningham, Rev. Thomas Finnegan, and Rev. Norman Thomas.

At the time of the article, Tony was directing the Pastoral Ministry program and Marygrove College, preparing lay men and women for ministry in the Church. *Human Sexuality*, which he co-authored with a group of theologians sponsored by the Catholic Theological Society of America and published in 1977, was described as "a radical departure from the official teachings of the Church."

Bill Cunningham was pastor of Madonna Parish in Highland Park. He was also the founder of Focus: HOPE, which continues to operate in the city as a program providing education and job training. The *News* article described the program as having "national prominence for giving its students a high-tech blend of classroom and on-the-job experience."

Tom Finnegan was pastor of St. Cecilia's parish, "a community church well-known for its basketball camp, which has produced such national standouts as New Jersey Nets forward Derrick Coleman, Golden State Warrior rookie Chris Webber and University of Michigan guard Jalen Rose."

Norm Thomas was pastor of Sacred Heart Parish in Detroit for many years until his death in 2023. In 1988, the Archdiocese of Detroit announced the closing of fifty city parishes. Through the efforts of Norm and the Detroit Catholic Pastoral Alliance (DCPA), twenty of these parishes remained open. Norm was credited with bringing "a lot of attention on the institution's failure to deal with racism." In this effort, he worked closely with other inner-city pastors, who supported one another and prayed together.

Bishop Tom Gumbleton, whom Tony highly respected and regarded as a friend, was ordained in 1956, the year following Tony's ordination class. He would appear to have absorbed the energy of the class before him in his own prophetic ministry to the underserved in many countries, his work in the peace movement, and especially his advocacy for nuclear disarmament. It is especially telling here that it was his personal testimony on behalf of clergy sex abuse victims in 2006 and 2007 that led to his removal from St. Leo's parish in Detroit, where he had been pastor for many years (Fromherz & Sattler, 2023).

Catholic Circles

The Detroit Catholic Pastoral Alliance (DCPA) hosted a Tuesday morning meeting, initially for a group of city pastors, which involved reading the Scriptures for the coming Sunday liturgy and reflecting on a question posed by one of the members of the group. This group included Tom

McAnoy and Bob Morand (Our Lady of the Rosary), Tom Gumbleton (St. Leo), Jerry Singer (Nativity of Our Lord), Tom Lumpkin (Dorothy Day House), John Markham (St. Elizabeth), Bob Kotlarz (Immaculate Heart of Mary), Tom Duffey (St. Patrick), Bob McGrath (St. Francis DeSales), Ron DeHondt (St. Gregory), David Preuss (OFM Cap) (St. Charles Borromeo), Ed Farrell (Sacred Heart Seminary), Tony Kosnik (Marygrove College), and John Nowlan (St. Hilary). By 1989, the group had expanded to include lay men and women, and women religious who ministered in these parishes, and priests from some of the suburban parishes. I was privileged to attend as a member and Minister of Service from Our Lady of the Rosary. The Ministers of Service, a kind of diaconate that included lay men and women from various city parishes, also came out of the Detroit Catholic Pastoral Alliance. Ministers of Service were especially active at Sacred Heart, in the city and on the altar during Sunday liturgies.

Tony had many friends. Some of his closest friends were women religious. This group included Sr. Anneliese Sinnott, OP, a close friend and colleague who held teaching and administrative roles at Sts. Cyril and Methodius Seminary, Marygrove College, and Ecumenical Theological Seminary; Sr. Yvonne Gellise, RSM, a close friend who held leadership roles in Mercy (now Trinity) health care settings and frequently consulted with Tony on health care ethics; and Sr. Liz Ozdych, a member of the Servants of Jesus and close friend, who provided invaluable help with the preparation of the *Human Sexuality* manuscript. These were important, sustaining and long-term friendships. These competent and highly educated women, together with many others, shared their perspectives on religious life with Tony over many years, contributing to his understanding of what it means to be a woman ministering in the Catholic Church. I think that he gained a deeper understanding of the frustrations, obstacles, and inequities that characterized their experience after he was forced to leave his teaching position at Orchard Lake seminary. Tony's later decision to marry represented a loss for many, perhaps felt most keenly by his closest friends. For Tony, it was a kind of leaving home. But it also meant that he moved into a very different way of life that meant a shift away from the shared experience of religious life. After Tony died in 2017, "crossed over," I also experienced something of this kind of loss. Our shared experience was profoundly changed. Oddly, this was something recognized by Sr. Agnes Cunningham, member of the Servants of the Holy Heart of Mary and one of the co-authors of *Human Sexuality*. I had not met her previously, but we had a brief phone conversation in January 2019 about my decision to write Tony's memoir. She was very supportive of my efforts. During our conversation, she also commented spontaneously that she had been thinking of me at Christmas time, what it must have meant for me to lose Tony.

Moral Theologians from the Catholic Tradition

Among scholars, Tony was also "in good company." He was part of a group of respected Catholic theologians and ethicists, who were formed in the Catholic tradition, but developed their thinking beyond the official Roman Catholic statements and teaching on the nature of sexuality and meaning of sexual relations. Official doctrine continues to reflect a strong emphasis on "act morality" and the pro-creative dimension of sex. These scholars have not adhered to official doctrine. The group includes several of Tony's contemporaries, Richard McCormick, SJ, Charles Curran, John McNeill, and Andre Guindon, as well as scholars who followed them, including Margaret Farley RSM, and Christine Gudorf. Members of this group have addressed a range of issues in the area of sexual ethics, including divorce and remarriage, artificial contraception, masturbation, as well as a broader commentary on Church teaching, such as dissent from non-infallible teaching and the understanding of natural law.

There are several important elements in the Catholic tradition that have allowed, and perhaps have led to, the development of the conceptualization of sexual ethics among members of this group. These include the primacy of Jesus' law of love, as well as a strong emphasis on justice for the poor and marginalized evident in his teaching. This leads to an emphasis on the relational aspects of sexuality and the development of a "personalist" perspective, described in Chapter 5. Moral questions then must consider what contributes to the full integration of the human personal-ity. In this approach, there is an emphasis on values, and a rejection of "act morality," implied in the official Church teaching. This means looking at a given behavior in light of its meaning for the individual, rather than condemning the behavior outright. For example, a kiss is not just a kiss. It may be an expression of affection, of passion, or it may represent betrayal.

Another important element in the Catholic tradition that has significance here is the development of a more dynamic understanding of natural law: "… the question is not whether the notion of natural law is appropriate; it is rather how it is to be interpreted, with what enrichment from behavioral sciences, with what theological perspectives" (McCormick, 1977, p. 564). Gudorf (1994) talks about natural law in terms of the "radical historicity of our world" (p. 74). "If we understand the nature of the human person as both integrated and embedded in a radically historical social situation, then natural law morality will also be historicized, and can no longer take the form of a code, or any longer direct humans to specific acts which are then understood as willed by God" (Gudorf, p. 72). This position, too, leads to a rejection of "act morality." Curran (1988, 2022) talks about historical consciousness in this regard, i.e. attending to the present reality, signs of the times. McCormick (1989) described a call for "a continued move from classical consciousness to historical consciousness" (p. 42) after Vatican II.

Perspectives on Church authority that make the distinction between "authoritative non-infallible teaching" (e.g. in the area of sexual morality) and "infallible teaching" (which pertains to doctrine) represent another important element. Curran (1988) has defended the right of Catholic theologians to dissent from non-infallible hierarchical teaching and has presented a more "cooperative and independent understanding" (p. 11) of the role of the theologian vis a vis the hierarchy. He took this stance in his opposition to the condemnation of artificial birth control in *Humanae Vitae* (Paul IV encyclical, July 1968). Curran maintained that *Humane Vitae* was not an infallible teaching. McCormick

(1989) emphasized the importance of dissent in searching out the truth, quoting Bernard Haring, who described dissent as "a prophetic ministry within the Church" (p. 36).

Finally, contemporary Scripture scholarship leads to serious questions about the official teaching of the magisterium in the area of sexual ethics. For example, nowhere in the New Testament does Jesus condemn homosexuality. Passages from the Old Testament are often taken out of historical context by more conservative individuals and groups and cited as evidence that God condemns same-sex relations. An example of this kind of misinterpretation is the Story of Sodom (Gn 19: 4-11). The Old Testament does not explicitly identify the sin of Sodom with homosexuality, but rather as a lack of justice (Isaiah 1:10; 3:9), or inhospitality (Wis. 10:8; 19:14). Gudorf (1994) talks about problems using Scripture and cites contradictory scriptural passages. She describes Scripture as "not only relevatory but also counter-relevatory, that not only are some direct scriptural imperatives and statements of theological fact mistaken but the message conveyed in countless stories is also false in terms of human experience of God" (p. 9). E.g., women viewed as property whose wellbeing was not considered important. Curran (1988) discusses the use and place of Scripture in moral theology as an important methodological question for moral theologians.

The following is a review of positions on same-sex relations and the LGBTQ community within the Catholic Church taken by this group of scholars, who have steered a rather unwieldy conversation about sexual ethics from a discussion of "act morality" to a discussion about what it means to be a whole human person and values that should govern all sexual activity. It is intended to give some context to specific issues addressed in *Human Sexuality*.

Richard McCormick, SJ, now deceased, was the John A. O'Brien Professor of Christian Ethics at the University of Notre Dame. McCormick called for the Church and those who minister in it to be a "liberating presence" to the "irreversibly homosexual" individual who is not called to celibacy (1989, p. 308). McCormick called for support and respect for LGBTQ individuals, as well as an end to discrimination by the Church or by secular society. This kind of "liberating presence" includes providing support to the individual in developing and living out "the qualities of the covenanted man-woman relationship through fidelity and exclusiveness" (p. 308). McCormick advocated full sacramental and social support by the Church and its ministers, and invited them to combat "all social, legal, and ecclesial discrimination against and oppression of the homosexual" (p. 308). He maintained that the evaluation of the irreversibility of one's sexual orientation and the question of call to celibacy comes out of an individual conscience decision. "The Church must acknowledge and respect that responsibility of conscience without trying to dictate its conclusions" (p. 309). McCormick took issue with the notion of "disordered" used in the *Declaration of Certain Questions Concerning Sexual Ethics* (Congregation for the Doctrine of the Faith, 1975). "It strikes me as being totally unnecessary to the defense of traditional Catholic conclusions about homosexual acts" (p. 311).

Charles Curran is a Catholic priest and moral theologian who is now retired from his position as Professor of Human Values at Southern Methodist University. In his earlier writing (1972), Curran provided what he termed a "compromise position" (p. 217) with regard to same-sex relations. Curran described heterosexual behavior in the context of marriage as the ideal but allowed that "... at times one may reluctantly accept homosexual unions as the only way in which some people can find a satisfying degree of humanity in their lives" (p. 217). Curran noted that the real moral problem in this area is not about heterosexual vs. same-sex relations, but rather "sex as a depersonalizing force vs. sex as the fulfillment of human relationship" (p. 211). In an interview with Tom Fox for the *National Catholic Reporter* in 2022, Curran noted that the social teaching of the Church changed and grew over the years. The sexual teaching of the Church, however, did not grow. Historical consciousness has not impacted this latter teaching, and the Church has been "unwilling to admit it was wrong."

John McNeill has described himself as a qualified and accredited theologian and an expert in sexual ethics. He is a former member of the Society of Jesus who left active ministry in 1987 and went on to work as a psychotherapist. McNeill (1976), like Curran, asserted that "the primary problem in sexual relationships is sex as a depersonalizing force vs. sex as a fulfillment of human relationship" (p. 195). Consistent with Tony's work in this area (described in *Human Sexuality*), McNeill took a personalist perspective on this issue. He asserted that same-sex relations are morally justified if they are "expressive of genuinely constructive human love" (p. 34). "I have posed the thesis that there is the possibility of morally good homosexual relationships and that the love which unites the partners in such a relationship, rather than alienating them from God, can be judged as uniting them more closely with God and as mediating God's presence in our world" (p. 195). McNeill suggested that Christian gays and lesbians within the Church are members of a marginalized and oppressed minority. He underscored the importance and value of dialogue between individuals engaging in same-sex relations, Church authorities, and the community as a means of raising consciousness about justice issues as they pertain to the homosexual community.

Andre Guindon, now deceased, was a Canadian theologian at St. Paul University, Ottawa. He took a broader societal perspective on same-sex relations. He began with a broader personalist stance: "... with the human fecundity approach, we focus on the task of each individual to grow, through the sexual language, into a whole self" (1986, p. 163). Guindon went on to raise the question of what gay fecundity brings to society: "... if it is an original source of humanization on its own terms in our society, then it should bring to the human sexual concert novel tonalities which enrich the quality of everyone's performance" (p. 163). He suggested the following "essential components of human sexual fecundity" (p. 163) found in same-sex relations:

Sensuous experience: "Partnered gay persons have the opportunity to deepen the sensuous experience and to liberate sensuality from the shame which weighs upon it" (p. 167).

Nonviolent style of partnership: "... lesbians and gays are in a unique position to liberate sexual relationships from stereotypical, aggressive styles and to develop an active, nonviolent style of partnership which we badly need at the present time if we want to survive as human beings" (p. 174).

Celebration of gratuitous love: "Gay persons whose sexual language is fruitful in faithfulness to a partner, in forgiveness towards their enemies, and in compassion for the oppressed have indeed mastered the art of sexual love in a way which can only guide Christian community" (p. 179).

Social sexual praxis: "The disquieting otherness of lesbians and gays plays a prophetic role to the extent that they are perceived as committed citizens" (p. 182). That is, gay and lesbian individuals—by virtue of their 'otherness'—are viewed as being in a position to challenge prevalent social sexual prejudices, such as "the widely held notion of heterosexual society that humanity is ultimately reconciled within the couple" (p. 185).

At the time of publication of *Human Sexuality: New Directions in American Catholic Thought,* commissioned by the Catholic Theological Society of America in 1977, Tony was an active priest of the Archdiocese of Detroit. He was professor of moral theology and dean at Sts. Cyril and Methodius Seminary, Orchard Lake, Michigan. He was chairperson of the group of authors who contributed to *Human Sexuality.* An important contribution of this work was to relativize the procreative dimension of sexuality, as but one aspect of the total reality, suggesting a broadening of the traditional formulation of the purpose of sexuality "from *procreative and unitive* to *creative and integrative*" (p. 86). The question of the morality of same-sex behavior per se was framed as a question of values for healthy relationships, presumed to foster creativity and integration. "Homosexuals have the same rights to love, intimacy, and relationships as heterosexuals. Like heterosexuals, they are also bound to strive for the same ideals in their relationships, for creativity and integration ... The norms governing the morality of homosexual activity are those that govern all sexual activity ..."

(p. 214). Sexual behavior that is "conducive to creative growth and integration of the human person, must be self-liberating, other-enriching, honest, faithful, socially responsible, life-serving, and joyous" (pp. 92-95).

The cost of dissent from official Church teaching for Tony and members of this group of scholars was high. Richard McCormick did not receive direct sanctions for his writings but was indirectly ignored for appointments on official Church committees, including the Bishops' Committee on Health Care issues (Kosnik, personal communication 2007). McCormick would have been considered to be an expert in this area. Charles Curran lost his mission to teach as a Catholic theologian in 1986 and was forced out of his position as Professor of Moral Theology at Catholic University. In 1974, the Congregation for the Doctrine of the Faith opened an inquiry into John McNeill's views about same-sex relations. He was silenced in 1977 and not permitted to speak about or minister to LGBTQ individuals. He refused to comply, and in 1986 the Society of Jesus began formal procedures to expel him. He left in 1987 to pursue a career as a psychotherapist. In 1992, Andre Guindon was notified that he was under investigation by the Congregation for the Doctrine of the Faith for his second book, *The Sexual Creators*, published in 1990. He was asked to clarify his views on same-sex relations, birth control, and premarital sex. Guindon died in 1993. It is interesting to note that in the introduction to his first book, *The Sexual Language*, published in 1976, Guindon asserted that he would "not take heed of irrational censorship" (p. 3). Tony was forced to leave his teaching position at Sts. Cyril and Methodius Seminary in Michigan in 1982 because of his work on *Human Sexuality: New Directions in American*

Catholic Thought, published in 1977. Tony refused to retract statements about masturbation and same-sex relations.

In spite of these efforts by the institution to silence these dissenting theologians, the conversation about sexual ethics has continued among Catholic scholars.

Christine Gudorf, Professor of Religious Studies at Florida International University and past president of the Society of Christian Ethics, published *Body, Sex, and Pleasure* in 1994. In this book, she has attempted to provide a broader perspective on sexuality and sexual ethics that integrates scientific understanding and "our understanding of the central revelations of the gospel" (1994, p.1). In her attempt at reconstruction of sexual ethics, she has also looked at the social context and social implications of sexual behavior. Gudorf has criticized the traditional approach to Christian sexual ethics in general, based on its failure to reflect justice and love, its "legalistic and apologetic approach" (p. 2), and the lack of serious consideration given to the general areas of scientific consensus regarding sexual issues. With regard to same-sex relations, Gudorf maintains that scientific understanding that sexual orientation is not chosen means that a same-sex orientation cannot be viewed as sinful, and this also raises questions about the "unnaturalness" of same-sex relations. She has endorsed an "appreciation—neither oppression nor mere tolerance—of gays and lesbians both for their distinctive individual gifts and for the insights their experience and perspective shed on humankind and God" (p. 25). Gudorf has criticized the "act morality" that is an important part of the traditional approach to sexual ethics, the idea that specific sexual behaviors are considered to be sinful. She has asserted instead that the quality of the relationship in which the behavior occurs and its consequences for the people involved are important in determining its morality. The body, sex, and pleasure are seen as God's gifts, revealing God's grace.

Margaret Farley RSM, who held the Gilbert L. Stark Chair in Christian Ethics at Yale University Divinity School, where she taught from 1971 to 2007, and is past president of the Society of Christian Ethics and the Catholic Theological Society of America, wrote *Just Love: A Framework for Christian Sexual Ethics*, published in 2006. Farley has listed the following "norms for sexual justice: 1. Do no unjust harm. 2. Free consent of partners. 3. Mutuality. 4. Equality. 5. Commitment. 6. Fruitfulness & Social Justice" (p. 231). These values are founded on "respect for the autonomy and relationality that characterize persons as end in themselves, and hence respect for their well-being, respect for auton- omy; respect for relationality; and respect for persons as sexual beings in society" (p. 231). With regard to same-sex relationships, "the key question is not whether same-sex relationships can be ethically justified but what must char- acterize these relationships when they are justified ... This sexual justice ethic is, in other words, an ethic for Christian— and perhaps all human—sexual relationships" (p. 288).

Some of the scholars cited above have contributed to the theological underpinnings of advocacy organizations for LGBTQ Catholics, including Dignity and New Ways Ministry. Dignity was founded by Patrick Nidorf OSA, an Augustinian priest and psychologist, as an extension of his work with gay Catholics. Dignity USA has become a national organization for LGBT Catholics, providing education, sup- port, and advocacy. Robert Nugent, a Salvatorian priest, and

Jeannine Gramick, formerly a School Sister of Notre Dame, now a Sister of Loretto, co-founded New Ways Ministry in 1977. The focus of their work has been on issues of pastoral care for gays and lesbians, and they have been involved in direct ministry (dialogue, counseling, celebrating home liturgies), as well as writing and lecturing in this area, and lobbying for legislation to secure gay rights.

New Ways Ministry was investigated by a Vatican Commission over a period of years, beginning in the early 1980s. Sr. Jennine Gramick reached out to Tony for advice and support during the course of this investigation, which was concluded in 1999. Sr. Gramick and Rev. Nugent were taken to task by the commission for their apparent failure "to respond unequivocally to certain questions regarding their position on the morality of homosexual acts and on the homosexual inclination," despite their efforts to present themselves as "an educational organization which takes no position, but which merely presents theological thinking on this topic" (Gramick, letter to Tony, April 1984). As a result of the investigation, Sr. Gramick and Rev. Nugent were permanently prohibited from "any pastoral work involving homosexual persons" and were also declared ineligible, "for an undetermined period for any office in their respective religious institutes" (Congregation for the Doctrine of the Faith, May 13, 1999). In spite of these efforts by the institution to silence Gramick and Nugent, New Ways Ministry has continued, and Jeannine Gramick is still involved in this work. In a letter to Cardinal Francis George, OMI, Archdiocese of Chicago, dated February 17, 2010, Tony responded to a statement made by the cardinal that "New Ways Ministry does not provide an authentic interpretation of Catholic teaching." This letter provides a glimpse of Tony's ongoing support for New Ways Ministry, as well as his advocacy and support for all of those sanctioned by the Church for following their "well-formed conscience."

> *The New Ways Ministry has rendered an incredible service to this persecuted group to which the official church offers no meaningful support. Quite to the contrary, the Church's official statements only further fuel the hatred and bigotry directed at this group. It is high time, I believe, that you and the official church get in touch with the Church's whole tradition and especially the pastoral care and sensitivity of Jesus whenever speaking to or about this group.*

Wider Circles

Tony wore his Roman Catholicism well throughout his life as he walked in wider and wider circles. He ostensibly left active ministry when we married, but he never really left it. His sense of inclusion, so evident in his round table ministry, and "preferential option for the poor" were deeply rooted.

After *Human Sexuality*, Tony did some writing, notably a chapter in *The Church in Anguish: Has the Vatican Betrayed Vatican II?* edited by Hans Kung and Leonard Swidler, published in 1986. Contributors to this book were Catholic theologians reflecting on attempts by the institutional church to undo the reforms of Vatican II. Under the protective pseudonym Adam Nowotny, Tony wrote a chapter entitled "Fortress Catholicism: Wojtyla's Polish Roots," a

critique of Pope John Paul II and his use of Church authority. Adam Nowotny was identified as "a pseudonym of an
expert in Polish religious affairs." "In Hebrew, *Adam* means
'human being' and in Polish, *nowotny* means 'new,'" (p. ix,
Contributors).

In his chapter, Tony noted that:

> [John Paul II's] *Polish messianism can prove to be
> an incredible source of strength, courage, and hope,
> provided it does not degenerate into a fanaticism
> that fails to distinguish between the divine will
> and one's own stubborn convictions. His desire to
> dispel the doubt and confusion regarding church
> doctrine disturbing so many of the faithful is well-
> intentioned, but if it insists on clarity and certitude
> where neither faith nor reason can guarantee such,
> his efforts will only provide a false security that
> prefers even the certitude of error to the ambiguity
> of reality. His strong sense of the importance of both
> solidarity and opposition to create a society where
> communal and individual needs are integrated will
> serve the church only if these attitudes are regarded
> as equally valid not only for civil society but for the
> church as well* (p. 37).

One of Tony's attempts to address the "ambiguity of reality" was a response to an op-ed piece in the *Detroit Free Press*
written by two professors at Sacred Heart Major Seminary
and a professor of law at Ave Maria School of Law in Ann
Arbor, Michigan (subsequently moved to Naples, Florida),
"Granholm's abortion stance is off base," October 17, 2002.
In the article, the authors maintained that Granholm's public

stance on abortion (pro-choice) was incompatible with her assertion that she was personally against abortion as a matter of her Catholic faith.

Tony had been active in the field of health care ethics throughout his active ministry. He served as consultant to the Advisory Committee of the American Bishops' Committee on Health Affairs and on the governing board of the Pope John XXIII Center for Medical-Moral Research and Education. He was also on the Task Force of Ethical Aspects of Genetic Diagnosis and Counseling of the Pope John XXIII Center. He served as a consultant in this area to a number of hospitals and health organizations. He continued to consult and teach in this area on issues such as end of life, after leaving active ministry. In his response to the op-ed, which was also signed by three priests from the Archdiocese of Detroit, Tony argued that "the question is a complex one and deserves more than a statement of condemnation in the most general terms" ("Priests defend Granholm," October 19, 2002, *Detroit Free Press*). He provided a more nuanced historical perspective regarding Church teaching on when life begins. He also reiterated the "recognized responsibility of individual Catholics to follow their well-formed consciences in making specific decisions." The letter added: *"When caught in conflicting values one must choose the course of action that will maximize the positive values and minimize the disvalues. An authentic respect for life must embrace a whole spectrum of issues affecting life including respect for freedom, housing, employment, education, nutrition, health care, etc. It is clear that in this decision Jennifer Granholm has chosen to follow her conscience. This is perfectly compatible with her responsibility as a Catholic and as a good citizen."*

Adam Cardinal Maida, then Archbishop of Detroit, took issue with the three priests who signed the document. In his letter to Rev. John Nowlan, one of the priests, he required a written apology for signing the document, a series of meetings with one of the auxiliary bishops to help clarify the Church's "sound doctrine" on the matter, and three days of retreat "to make reparation for the harm [you] have done and to ask for the help of the Holy Spirit in dispelling the confusion in your thinking."

Wider Circles: Catholic Groups

Elephants in the Living Room: What Needs to be Discussed came out of a conversation that took place at a convocation for priests of the Archdiocese of Detroit held at Boyne Mountain, Michigan in October 2003. During a general meeting at the convocation, Rev. Gerry Bechard asked Cardinal Maida whether they were going to talk about the "elephant in the living room." According to his report, the question was ignored. Several of the priests present got together and decided that there were issues that needed to be discussed when they returned to Detroit. They agreed to hold meetings for that purpose. In the by-laws of the Elephants, the group is described as "an organization of priests of the Archdiocese of Detroit, strongly supported by participating laity, who seek renewal of the Church of Detroit. Our purpose is to offer opportunities for education and creating an open forum for discussion and dialog that will lead to developing and advocating more collegial solutions to the challenges we face." Membership has included Catholic clergy, religious, and lay persons. Educational forums have included: Ecclesiology of Vatican II (Rev. Michael Himes), Evolving Visions of the Priesthood (Dean Hoge), Need for Reform of Church Structures (Tom Fox), Critical Issues Facing the Church (Rev. Richard McBrien), Women in the Church (Sr. Joan Chittister), and Priestly Celibacy and the Future (Rev. Donald Cozzens). Bishop Tom Gumbleton was active in this group. He invited and introduced the speakers. Rev. Tom Lumpkin has also maintained a leadership role. Tony was presented with the Bishop Gumbleton award by the Elephants on June 2, 2007, for his work with this group. He was given a plaque and an elephant as part of this award. The elephant continues to inhabit my living room.

Michigan Catholics for the Common Good[1] is a group directed at social reform. The mission of this group is "to promote, within our local dioceses and parishes, the fundamental principle of Catholic social teaching: respect for the dignity and sacredness of every person. Through this principle, we will work to combat divisiveness, fear tactics, or untruths promoted by church leaders and commit to address issues of racism and discrimination, environmental degradation, immigration, poverty, and more." Tony was very active in Catholics for the Common Good, involved in both planning and presenting on Catholic social teaching in various parishes of the archdiocese. "Single issue voting" and conscience formation were among the important topics presented. We hosted many planning meetings around our dining room table. As Tony had more difficulty getting around at the end of his life, the group met regularly at our home so that he could continue his leadership role.

---

1 MichiganCatholicsForCommonGood.org

In March 2011, Tony did an invited presentation, "Ethics and Politics: an Oxymoron?" at Oakland Community College, which came out of his work with Catholics for the Common Good. In his talk, Tony reflected on the "profound disconnect" between ethics, *the science which deals with the nature of the human being ... what it means to be human and what one ought to do*, and politics, *the science that deals with the question: How do we bring this incredibly rich and diverse community of God's people into a harmonious whole?* In this talk, Tony applied Catholic social teaching to his analysis of the political turmoil evident in American society. He cited the widening gap between the rich and the poor, people from the middle and lower classes pushed out, or left out, of the American mainstream as the "most important and potentially the most dangerous issue facing the country." He pointed to legislation and public policies that supported these inequities and asserted that America was founded on democratic principles that translate into respect and dignity for all people. So it was time to work for change. At this time in his life, Tony was looking at the world around him from the vantage point of someone in it, someone who now had to figure out mortgage payments, groceries, and health insurance in a way that was different from before. He had stepped out of a more privileged role as ordained minister in the Catholic Church.

Ecumenical Circles

Tony was one of the first members of the faculty of **Ecumenical Theological Seminary,**[2] described on its

2 ETSeminary.edu

website as providing "a multi-confessional Christian Theological education within an urban context, while initiating interfaith engagement. Our approach creates spiritual leadership through personal transformation, social responsibility, critical reflection, and academic rigor. ETS graduates are prepared to lead communities of faith while sharing God's compassion in relationship to various ecumenical, interfaith, political, social, economic, and cultural contexts." ETS is based in Detroit, "a unique laboratory for ministerial education." In addition to his teaching responsibilities, Tony served as Interim Director of the Doctor of Ministry program in 1997-98. In these roles, he was involved in training ministers from various Christian denominations. Tony was recognized as Professor Emeritus in June 2000 upon his retirement from ETS.

Wranglers was another, perhaps more informal, ecumenical group. Membership consisted of individuals from various Christian denominations, who came together on a periodic basis to "wrangle" about scholarly theological issues. Tony made a presentation to this group in April 2011, "Theology or Ideology?" In his talk to this group, he posed the question: When does a theological position become "ideology," and what is it that makes it so? *My initial assumption is that there are two characteristics that make this possible: the first is to claim as absolute the primary principle (value, or position) one is espousing. And secondly, to refuse to be open to any new insights, additional information, or new perspectives that might modify that position.* He went on to talk about examples from the field of ethics, positions from the Catholic tradition, that appeared to be more ideological then theological, issues of birth control, same-sex relations, and the Church's response to clerical pedophilia. He also discussed the official position of the Catholic Church on the role of other religions in salvation, and quoted John Paul II: "... the salvific role of Jesus Christ is unique and singular, proper to him alone, exclusive, universal and absolute." Tony then quoted theologian Elizabeth Johnson from Catholic University (*Quest for the Living God*), who has maintained that other religions can, by God's design, open our minds and hearts to new ways of thinking. Tony noted, *I see other signs of hope all around us in the increasing Interfaith Groups that have arisen in recent years, in the ongoing Catholic Muslim dialogue, the Jewish Catholic Dialogue, and the much greater cooperation taking place among these groups on social, political, and charitable issues.*

In the late 1980s, Tony was involved in the **Greater Detroit Interfaith Round Table**, which sponsored two meetings of Christian, Muslim, and Jewish leaders at Marygrove College, directed at helping to lessen religious prejudice. The second meeting was a conference, "Respect and Reconciliation Among the Abrahamic Religions." "The fact that all three faiths look back to Abraham as a patriarch and find many other parallels in their scriptures, provides the shared basis for discussion" (David Crumm, *Detroit Free Press*, Oct. 28, 1987). As he stated in his 2011 talk for the Wranglers (above), Tony saw these meetings as important opportunities for dialogue, *limiting our ideological tendencies and developing a theology that more truly reflects God's design for our world.*

Reporters and Grandchildren

For Tony, any discussion about The Company You Keep would be incomplete without recognizing the reporters who chronicled his adventures, or the young grandchildren with whom he lived for the last five years of his life. Reverend Harry Cook, an Episcopal priest, was a member of the first group. Harry worked for the *Detroit Free Press* as religion reporter, editor, and columnist during the period when Tony was experiencing fallout related to the publication of *Human Sexuality*. In Tony's papers regarding the book were a long series of carefully clipped news articles—each with Harry Cook's byline. Harry was a force in his own right, with a passion for social justice and a deep love for his own family. In the last years of Tony's life, we would run into Harry and his wife, Sue Chevalier, at the grocery store, and at Our Lady of Fatima, where we all attended Mass. Harry and Tony died within three weeks of each other. I imagine that they are now enjoying some great conversations about theology and family life. David Crumm is another member of this group. David was also a religion writer for the *Detroit Free Press* who followed Tony's involvement in the Greater Detroit Interfaith Roundtable, and who shepherded me through the throes of this memoir to its eventual publication. These journalists might be viewed as part of the "great cloud of witnesses" by whom Tony was (and we are) surrounded (Hebrews, 12:1).

My two young grandchildren came to live with us in 2012, when they were six and ten. Tony never questioned their need to live with us, nor the length of their stay. They had their own spaces in our house (and often usurped our spaces, too). They were part of Tony's Christmas letter from the first year. Living with young children forces one to look at what is really important, and to confront one's limitations daily. 'What is for dinner?' 'When do we go for ice cream?' 'Why is Jesus on the cross on that big church?' (Shrine of the Little Flower, Royal Oak, Michigan) 'Read me another story.' 'Let's wrestle, Papa.'

This kind of dialogue adds perspective.

2d interfaith talks seek greater understanding

By DAVID CRUMM
Free Press Religion Writer

About 200 Christian, Muslim and Jewish leaders will be on common ground today at Marygrove College in Detroit, building on a historic meeting last year that showed their differences could be discussed with a minimum of fireworks.

"Last year we just had to prove we could do it; this year we can use the program as a launching pad for broadening the experience," said David Jaffe, president of the American Jewish Committee's Detroit chapter.

The conference has been promoted by the Greater Detroit Interfaith Round Table as an opportunity for pastors and lay people to form bonds that may help to lessen religious prejudice.

Last year, planners feared that protesters would gather at the first conference, but none did. Only one of nine workshops, a session on the effects of terrorism, erupted in shouting.

The Rev. Alex Brunett, director of interreligious affairs for the Catholic Archdiocese of Detroit, said the conferences may be unique in the country.

"Where in the United States can you find religious leaders — Jewish, Christian and Muslim — getting together at the same conference? Nowhere except in highly controlled academic settings," Father Brunett said. "These are pastors and lay people and it's a great

A WORLD OF DIFFERENCE

the American Muslim Bekaa Center in Dearborn, said: "It is very helpful and makes us come together to learn more about each other. . . . We have a lot of common things between the religions. We are Abrahamic religions."

The conference title, "Respect and Reconciliation Among the Abrahamic Religions," was chosen by the Muslim, Christian, Jewish Leadership Forum, an offshoot of the Round Table formed specifically to organize the conferences.

The fact that all three faiths look back to Abraham as a patriarch and find many other parallels in their scriptures, provides the shared basis for discussion.

Progress is slow in interfaith work, said Jaffe, but the Abrahamic conferences represent progress nonetheless. "It's another piece of the puzzle in a kind of work that doesn't come about in giant leaps. You don't erase 2,000

Controversial priest quits

By HARRY COOK
Free Press Religion Writer

A Catholic priest who wrote a controversial book on human sexuality five years ago has resigned his professorship at St. Cyril and Methodius Seminary in Orchard Lake. Sources say the resignation results from a move to stifle the liberal theological ideas he espoused.

The Rev. Anthony Kosnik, 52, professor of moral theology at the Orchard Lake seminary, told the faculty Monday that he was resigning effective July 1.

A spokesman for Father Kosnik said the priest "was not making himself available to the press." However, the seminary's rector, the Rev. Francis B. Koper, confirmed that Father Kosnik had resigned but dismissed reports that the resignation was forced.

A SOURCE close to the situation said the Rev. Stanley Milewski, an official of the Orchard Lake school, and the Most Rev. Edmund C. Szoka, Catholic archbishop of Detroit, recently urged Father Kosnik to leave the seminary. Neither Archbishop Szoka nor Father Milewski could be reached for comment.

Father Kosnik is one of five Catholics who published "Human Sexuality: New Directions in American Catholic Thought" in 1977.

The book, which caused a furor in the Catholic Church, said that there was no explicit moral prohibition of masturbation, that a blanket condemnation of pre-marital sex is no longer taken seriously by most American Catholics and that homosexuals should be dealt with gently by the church. Vatican officials in 1979 urged the authors to "correct their errors."

A SOURCE told the Free Press Tuesday that Father Kosnik "has long been a target of the conservatives in the church and has apparently fallen victim to a purge that will involve more people than just (Father) Kosnik."

Another source said several faculty members at the seminary "have threatened to resign in protest of what they see as a totally unnecessary resignation, one that was demanded. Tony's friends are being rallied to support him."

Several weeks ago a committee of clergy visited the Orchard Lake campus as part of a nationwide study and evaluation of the church's 501 U.S. seminaries, ordered last year by Pope John Paul II.

A friend of Father Kosnik's quoted the priest as saying he had been grilled by the committee about his part in writing the book on human sexuality. "I'm sure that's how all this came down," the friend said.

Top left: David Crumm byline, *Detroit Free Press*, 1986.

Top right: Harry Cook byline, *Detroit Free Press*, 1982.

Left: The elephant in our living room, which accompanied the Bishop Gumbleton award given to Tony by the Elephants in the Living room in 2007.

Top: Rev. Norm Thomas at the table, celebrating Tony's fiftieth anniversary of ordination.

Bottom: Around the table, celebration of the fiftieth
anniversary of ordination, St. John class of 1955.

Top: Celebrating Tony's fiftieth anniversary of ordination.

Bottom: This is a New Year's Day celebration, held annually by a group of Mercy sisters. Sister Yvonne Gellise is seated at the far left in front.

Top: Tony and Peg with grandchildren, 2008.

Bottom: This photo was taken on the occasion of Tony's sixty-fifth birthday. Left to right, back to front: Sister Anneliesa Sinnott, O.P., Tony, Rev. Robert Werenski, Bev Sinke, Peggy, Sister Liz Ozdych, Sister Jo Gaugier, O.P.

8

Other Voices

Bidden or not bidden, God is present.
Carl Jung

Early in my career as a social scientist, I found my own faith seriously tested in light of the dismissal of my professional training in areas such as sexual orientation, gender identity, normative sexual behavior (e.g. masturbation), as well as a wider disdain for the scientific method by the Catholic Church. It was in my early conversations with Tony that I found that I could be intellectually honest and maintain my belief in God and participation in the Church. He introduced me to the writings of theologians, such as those discussed in the preceding chapter, who maintained a broader under-standing of natural law, and who took a variety of positions on moral issues which were at odds with the institutional Church. In those early days of my relationship with Tony, I wrote the following poem:

Preacher

Healer
Prophet
Saver of Souls
Fisher of Men
Into the dark night
You cast your nets
and wait
with infinite patience
and certainty of your
catch, drawn
by a faint and distant glimmering.

In the first light
I can almost see
that you are not alone in the boat.

Dr. Francis Collins, widely known scientist and director of the Human Genome Project, wrote *The Language of God* (2006), a book in which he recounts his own journey from atheism to agnosticism to belief. The Catholic church has a long history of dismissing scientists, notably Galileo, Copernicus, Darwin, and many others. And much worse. But scientists haven't all dismissed God. And many did not leave their church. Collins says that, in the end, there is no logical proof of God's existence. But he was persuaded to start his journey to belief during medical school, through his encounters with his most suffering patients—who did believe, "whose faith provided them with a strong reassurance of ultimate peace, be it in this world or the next, despite terrible suffering ..." (p. 19). Collins goes on to talk about what he views as the universality of Moral Law, and about his sense of a just and loving God. He notes that "science is not threatened by God; it is enhanced. God is most certainly not threatened by science; [God] made it possible" (p. 233).

For a number of years, during my tenure at the University of Detroit Mercy, I taught a class entitled Religion and Psychology. It was listed as an undergraduate class, but I would also have a few graduate students who enrolled. At the start of each term, I asked students about their religious affiliation. The course did attract students from different religious traditions, but the biggest number always seemed to be disaffected Catholics, students who would describe their upbringing as Catholic but now saw themselves as "spiritual" or non-believing or searching. In my introductory lecture for this class, I talked about methods, for science and for theology. I think that this discussion is important here. What I'll do with this chapter is to review the evidence from the social sciences for the issues raised in *Human Sexuality*. Doing so requires a review of methodology in the social sciences, as well as a comparison of scientific method and theological method.

The social sciences and theology represent different disciplines directed at understanding human experience. Kenneth Pargament, a researcher and clinical psychologist who has conducted extensive research on religion (theological studies) and psychology (as representative of the social sciences), draws a distinction between these disciplines: Psychology may be seen as a profession that attempts to help people gain more control over what they have not controlled, which could include making behavioral changes, or gaining insight. Religion helps people appreciate what they cannot control. That is, religion offers a way to come to terms with the limitations of material goods, personal desires, and other limits through frameworks of belief that go beyond control (Pargament, 2001, pp. 7-8). Pargament suggests enriching religion through psychological study, and enriching psychology through religion. "To ignore the findings of science is theologically irresponsible and to ignore the deeper impulses of the human spirit is scientifically suicidal" (Pargament, p. 13).

From a social science perspective, questions about human behavior and/or mental processes might include: What is normative? Under what conditions does a given behavior occur? What are possible pathways to a given condition, like mental illness, behavioral disturbance, resilience, adaptive coping, marital satisfaction, or other issue? Theories may be generated based on single case observations and then tested through research. The research process involves the following steps:

1. Identify and analyze the problem to be studied.

2. Generate hypotheses (predictions) about behavior.

3. Develop a method for systematic observation.

4. Obtain a representative sample of people to be studied, i.e. a (smaller) group of people who display the characteristics of the (larger) group one wishes to study.

5. Collect data, i.e. quantify observations.

6. Apply statistical analysis.

7. Draw inferences.

There are a variety of research methods for systematic observation. These include the experimental method, which involves the manipulation of variables to find cause and effect relationships between variables; correlational studies, which look at the relationship between variables, in terms of both strength and direction of relationship; and case studies, which involve an in-depth analysis of individual cases. Often the individual case study is used as a starting point to generate research questions. There are limitations on how much we can observe. For example, internal experience (feeling) might need to be inferred. And it is often difficult to sort out the complexity of factors that influence behavior, although newer research methodology is improved because it considers this complexity by using multiple regression, structural equation modeling, and other methods.

Theological methods include both deductive and inductive approaches. In a deductive approach, Scripture or sacred writings are interpreted literally and considered to have the truth. Sources are applied, and conclusions drawn. The question one asks—coming from this perspective—is "What should my experience be, based on the sacred sources?" This approach would be characteristic of the more fundamentalist Christian traditions. An inductive theological approach makes use of multiple sources: Scripture/sacred writings, tradition, science/reason, spirit, and experience. Coming from this perspective, one asks "Does [the source] have something to say about my experience?" or "What does the source have to say about my experience?" Then experience is examined in light of the sources (Kosnik, personal communication). *Human Sexuality* (Kosnik, et. al., 1977) makes use of this kind of inductive approach.

All of this method does not exist in a vacuum. Questions that are raised for study in both disciplines come out of theoretical perspectives. Or, theory guides the questions, directs our course of study. Natural law, discussed in the preceding chapter, would be a starting point for theology. What is the nature of the human person? Curran's (2006) distinction between classicism and historical consciousness in approaches to understanding natural law provides a clear summary of these approaches. "Classicism emphasizes the eternal, immutable, and unchanging. Human nature is the same at all times and in all places" (p. 30). This position is characteristic of traditional Catholic teaching. "Historical consciousness, by contrast, emphasizes the particular, the historical, the individual, and the contingent" (p. 30). *Human Sexuality* (Kosnik et al.) utilizes this more dynamic understanding of natural law.

Coming out of this understanding of natural law, Kosnik et al. emphasize the relational aspects of sexuality.

> It can be said that sexuality serves the development of human persons by calling them to constant creativity, that is, to full openness to being, to the realization of every potential within the personality, to a continued discovery and expression of authentic selfhood. Procreation is one form of this call to creativity but by no means is it the only reason for sexual expression. Sexuality further

serves the development of genuine personhood by calling people to a clearer recognition of their relational nature, of their absolute need to reach out and embrace others to achieve personal fulfillment. Sexuality is the Creator's ingenious way of calling people constantly out of themselves into relationship with others (Kosnik et al., 1977, p. 85).

Moral questions then must consider what contributes to the full integration of the human personality. In this approach, there is an emphasis on values, and a rejection of "act morality," described in Chapter 6.

In the social sciences, this dynamic understanding of natural law and the personalist perspective are reflected in humanistic, object relations, and attachment theories. From a humanistic perspective, the human person is viewed as having potential for positive growth. The assumption is that there is an intrinsic goodness to human nature, and that under optimal conditions, individuals will develop their potential. Maslow has suggested that we have a hierarchy of needs, and that our "lower order needs," including physiological needs, safety, love, belonging, and esteem must be satisfied if a person is to reach their potential. "Self-actualization" (Maslow, 1970) and the "fully functioning person" (Rogers, 1961) are terms used to describe this realization of potential. Characteristics of the fully functioning person include openness to experience, mindfulness (living fully in each moment), reliance on inner experience to guide behavior, experience of freedom to choose, and creativity

(Rogers). This perspective looks at the whole human person, in context.

Object relations theory considers the development of the whole human person in the context of relationship with another person. The first relationship is with the primary caregiver or caregivers, but the circle expands over the course of development to include other relationships. From this perspective, human experience and behavior derive fundamentally from the search for and maintenance of contact with others. Attachment theory has been described by John Bowlby as a variant of object relations theory. Bowlby (1988) viewed the child's tie to a caregiver as the result of a distinctive set of behavior patterns which, in the "ordinary expectable environment," develop during the early months of life and have the effect of keeping the child in more or less close proximity to his or her mother figure. Attachment theory explains these patterns of proximity-seeking behavior, leading to the development of positive emotional bonds, as characteristic not only of infants and small children but also adolescents and adults. This propensity to develop intimate emotional bonds is viewed as a basic component of human nature and is an important foundation for healthy emotional functioning and healthy relationships. (See Xing Zhang et al., 2022, for a comprehensive review of the literature on attachment outcomes.)

As reported in an earlier chapter, the Committee on Doctrine (NCCB) referred to Kosnik's list of values "conducive to creative growth and integration of the human person." The values, self-liberating, other-enriching, honest, faithful, socially responsible, life-serving, and joyous, were described as "second level values" which "offer little guidance" (p. 4) in the committee's critique of *Human Sexuality*. This critique is not supported by research on marital and other committed relationship outcomes.

Self-liberating, other-enriching, honest, faithful

The capacity to engage in reciprocal give-and-take adult relationships is critical for successful long-term marriages. Higher marital satisfaction is associated with the couple's quality of communication and cooperative conflict management style (Bertoni & Bodenmann, 2010). Honesty is critical to quality of communication. Other process variables associated with the quality of marital relationships include commitment, loyalty, and forgiveness (Fawcett et al, 2013). These might be viewed as more transformative processes that enhance the quality of marital relationships. Kindness is an important transformative variable associated with marital satisfaction (Selcuk & Imamoglu, 2018; Weisfeld, Weisfeld, & Goetz, 2018). In a cross-cultural study, Dillon et al. (2015) found that kindness was associated with reduced marital conflict across five different cultures. Infidelity is associated with marital and sexual dissatisfaction (Allan, 2004).

Socially responsible, life-serving

When Tony's brother Bernie told me that I would be marrying the whole family (prior to our marriage), he was reminding me that marriage has a social context that goes beyond the individual partners. The couple needs the support of the wider family and community and also has an

impact on the wider family and community. The terms
"socially responsible" and "life-serving" speak to this complicated relationship. Social networks and religious institutions
serve as "important sources of social structural support for
marriage" (Wilcox & Dew, 2010). This means that the couple's union is recognized by the community, which can also
provide various forms of support during times of difficulty
and may offer models of stable and successful marriages.
The couple then becomes part of a community that provides
these supports for other couples. Kearns & Leonard (2004)
suggest that there may be a "reciprocal influence between
[social] network interdependence and marital quality," or
"positive marital adjustment" (p. 393). High social support in
"love marriages" is reported to be related to marital harmony
(Kaur & Bhargava, 2016). Arifain et al. (2021) suggest that
social support is related to marital satisfaction for working
women.

The term "life-serving" is related to a sense of purpose
and/or meaning in a marriage. This may include having
and raising children for some couples, although for other
couples, this "creative and integrative" dimension may take
other forms. Research on "sanctification" and marriage
best captures the meaning of this construct. This refers to
couples viewing their marriage as somehow of God, perceiv-
ing the manifestation of God in the marriage and having a
sense of the holiness and sacredness of marriage (Mahoney
et al., 2010). Lichter & Carmalt (2009) found that viewing
one's marriage as sanctified was related to higher marital
satisfaction and commitment for husbands and wives. In
a qualitative study, Dollahite & Lambert (2007) reported
a connection between sanctification of the marriage and

higher marital quality, "which indirectly promoted fidelity" (p. 290). In national and community samples, sanctification of marriage has been connected to higher marital quality (Mahoney, 2010; Mahoney, Pargament and DeMaris, 2009), and increased marital satisfaction (Ellison et al., 2011; Stafford et al, 2014).

Joyous

The Song of Songs in the Old Testament is a poetic reflection on the joy experienced by romantic partners. In the social science literature, this construct has been presented in drier and more clinical terms, but still highlights its importance for romantic partners. In his book, *What Predicts Divorce: The Relationship Between Marital Processes and Marital Outcomes*, Gottman (2023) reviews his own and others' extensive research in this area. He maintains that the ratio of positivity to negativity in a couple's interactions has important implications for marital stability and satisfaction. This does not mean that there is no conflict, but rather that conflict has the potential to create "a dynamic equilibrium that has the capacity for change, adaptation, and renewal" (p. 414). Negativity that works against the stability of a marriage includes criticism, contempt, defensiveness, and withdrawal.

A related construct is the study of humor and its implications for marital satisfaction. Humor has been found to be positively related to marital satisfaction (De Koning & Weiss, 2000). Hall (2015) found that humor production was related to perceived warmth. Humorousness has been reported to be related to kindness, understanding, and dependability, and humor production "may actively strengthen a marriage by indicating an intention to be kind, understanding, and dependable—to be committed to the marriage" (Weisfeld, 2018, p. 246).

Overall, it would appear that this list of values presented in *Human Sexuality* (1977) is supported by extensive research on romantic partnerships. This has implications for long-term committed relationships, i.e. marriage. It should be noted that "the relational components of gay and lesbian couples are remarkably similar to those of heterosexual couples ... sexual orientation may have little to no bearing on the core aspects that human beings find important and fulfilling in their romantic relationships" (Weisfeld, Silveri, & Fedon-Keyt, 2018, p. 159).

Research on sexual orientation

What do we understand about pathways to sexual orientation? Today's twenty-first century conversation would be about acceptance and support of LGBTQ individuals, gender identity, the gender binary and understanding oneself outside of the gender binary, cisgender, transgender identities. Gender identity, one's private and personal perception of gender, is the issue of concern.

But today's conversation started with a discussion about sexual orientation, same-sex orientation. Kinsey might be given credit for beginning our more public conversations about sexual behavior. He published *Sexual Behavior in the Human Male* in 1948, and *Sexual Behavior in the Human Female* in 1953. These were exhaustive reports about sexual behaviors of American men and women, based on thousands of sexual histories that he and his colleagues obtained over two decades, beginning in the 1930s. In terms of prevalence of non-heterosexual orientation, Kinsey reported that 10% of their sample of white men had been "exclusively homosexual" for at least a three-year period in their lives and that 1% to 3% of women were "predominantly or exclusively homosexual." Other more recent nationally representative surveys indicate that approximately "2.5% to 7% of American men and women self-identify as homosexual or bisexual" (reported in King & Regan, 2019, p. 214). We can also say that sexual orientation is not associated with psychopathology (Hooker, 1957). These findings were replicated in subsequent studies. (See Bell & Weinberg, 1978 for a review of these studies, pp. 197-98.) In 1973, the American Psychiatric Association discontinued its classification of homosexuality as a mental illness. The American Psychological Association subsequently endorsed this position.

The DSM-5 (American Psychiatric Association, 2013) provides the following definition of "mental disorder," or psychopathology:

> A mental disorder is a syndrome characterized by clinically significant disturbance in an individual's cognition, emotion regulation, or behavior that reflects a dysfunction in the psychological, biological, or developmental processes underlying mental functioning. Mental disorders are usually associated with significant distress or disability in social, occupational, or other important activities. An expectable or culturally approved response to a common stressor or loss, such as the death of a

loved one, is not a mental disorder. Socially deviant behavior (e.g., political, religious, or sexual) and conflicts that are primarily between the individual and society are not mental disorders unless the deviance or conflict results from a dysfunction in the individual, as described above. (p. 20)

Sexual orientation does not meet the criteria for this kind of classification.

At the time of publication of *Human Sexuality* in 1977, sexual orientation and acceptance and support of individuals with a same-sex orientation were important concerns—and a point of contention between the Congregation for the Doctrine of the Faith and the group of Catholic moral theologians (Kosnik, Curran, etc.), whose positions were described in the last chapter. The official Roman Catholic statements on sexuality, which encompass the nature of sexuality and meaning of sexual relations, continue to reflect a strong emphasis on the procreative dimension of sex. These teachings are summarized in a document developed in 1975 by the CDF, *Declaration on Certain Questions Concerning Sexual Ethics*. Divine revelation, sacred scripture, and the Church's interpretation of natural law are cited as foundation for "... its traditional teaching that only in legitimate marriage does the use of the sexual faculty find its true meaning and probity" (p. 378). The document characterizes sexual relations between persons of the same sex as "necessarily and essentially disordered according to the objective moral order" (p. 381). It goes on to depict all violations of sexual morality (including same-sex sexual relations) as "objectively grave" (p. 384). Same-sex behavior is viewed as intrinsically evil. While the non-heterosexual orientation itself is not viewed as sinful, the only positive moral option offered the individual is that of celibacy.

From a social science perspective, this position is problematic on a number of fronts. First of all, sexual orientation does not appear to be a dichotomous variable. Based on his data, Kinsey proposed a 7-point scale, "in which 0 represented exclusive heterosexuality and 6 represented exclusive homosexuality ... 3 on the scale indicated equal homosexual and heterosexual responsiveness" (Coleman, 1988, p. 10). This scale allows that one might be bisexual, or sexually attracted to both men and women. Other researchers have suggested that this construct is multidimensional and includes sexual/romantic attraction, sexual behavior, and sexual identity, or self-definition as gay, lesbian, bisexual, or heterosexual person (Savin-Williams, 2006; Hines, 2011). Many people show variability across these dimensions. Hines (2011) notes, "it is clear that there is a good deal of within sex variability in sexual orientation, and that a substantial minority of both sexes have some erotic interest in individuals of their own sex" (p. 170).

For non-heterosexual males who show consistency across these dimensions, researchers have identified several different pathways to sexual orientation. One pathway involves genetic factors. Hamer et al. (1993) have provided data to suggest that "at least one subtype of male sexual orientation is genetically influenced" (p. 321). Swift-Gallant et al. (2019) cite studies suggesting that "a well-established biomarker of sexual orientation is familiality of male same-sex sexual orientation. Same-sex orientation clusters in families, twin studies show greater sexual orientation concordance among monozygotic (identical) than dizygotic (fraternal) twins, and molecular genetic studies have identified candidate genes associated with sexual orientation" (p. 12,787).

Swift-Gallant et al. (2019) have described handedness as a "well-studied biomarker of sexual orientation." "A large body of evidence indicates that non-right-handedness is more common among gay men than among heterosexual men, suggesting that at least some proportion of gay men owe their same-sex sexual orientation to developmental mechanisms underlying handedness" (p. 12,788).

Another pathway to same-sex sexual orientation appears to be related to the effects of prenatal hormone exposure. There are no apparent hormonal differences in adulthood between men and women who are heterosexual and those who are not (Hines, 2011). Sexual differentiation in humans and other mammals can be attributed to prenatal exposure to testicular hormones (i.e. antigens). This exposure during a critical or sensitive period in fetal development causes "male-typical" development. In the absence of testicular hormones "female-typical" development occurs (Hines, 2011). Fraternal birth order studies have examined the effect of prenatal hormonal influences on development of same-sex sexual orientation. Across a variety of cultures and samples, older brothers increase the odds that later-born males will show a same-sex sexual orientation. The explanation for this is that, with successive pregnancies, the mother may be producing antibodies to male antigens (Blanchard, 2017; Swift-Gallant et al, 2019). Studies on maternal stress during pregnancy have also looked at the effect of prenatal hormonal influences on sexual orientation in men, suggesting that stress may alter the production of prenatal androgens (Dorner,

1983). Subsequent studies of maternal stress reported retrospectively have yielded mixed results. For women, there is some evidence showing "altered sexual orientation" related to exposure to high levels of androgens prenatally because of congenital adrenal hyperplasia (Meyer-Bahlberg, Dolezal, & Baker, 2008).

Conversion therapy

The pathways to same-sex sexual orientation for men are better understood and clearer than for women, who show more variability. All of these possible pathways to same-sex sexual orientation, however, point to the importance of very early biological influences on development. Research has not supported the belief that sexual orientation is strongly influenced by early childhood experiences and/or the sexual orientation of one's parents (Garnets, 2002). It is worth repeating here that there is a good deal of variability among men and women across the dimensions of sexual orientation, sexual/romantic attraction, sexual behavior, and sexual identity.

Conversion therapy, which purports to change sexual orientation, has made use of behavioral techniques to try to change or alter same-sex gender attraction and behavior. Conversion therapy practices have been described as "organized and sustained efforts to avoid the adoption or expression of lesbian, gay, bisexual, or queer (LGBQ) sexual orientations, gender identities not assigned at birth, and/or non-conforming gender expressions" (Salway et al., 2021). These interventions have been shown to be ineffective and harmful. (See Campbell et al., 2023; Streed et al., 2019; Salway et al., 2021; Trispiotis & Purshouse, 2021 for extensive reviews of conversion therapies and outcomes.) "Conversion therapy is rooted in the notion that any nonheterosexual sexual orientation is a pathology in need of a 'cure'" (Streed et al., 2019). Professional medical associations, including the American Psychiatric Association and the American Psychological Association, have publicly denounced conversion therapy, which has been banned for minors in a number of states. The practice has been associated with both physical and mental health risks for LGBTQ individuals.

Impact of traditional Church teaching on sexuality

The research studies cited here certainly raise questions about classicism as an approach to understanding natural law, which provides the foundation for traditional Catholic teaching on sexuality. It does not appear that "human nature is the same at all times and in all places" (Curran, p. 30). In their book, *The Sexual Person: Toward a Renewed Catholic Anthropology* (2008), Salzman & Lawler have provided a comprehensive critique of this ahistorical interpretation of human nature (p. 235).

For the writers of *Human Sexuality*, the larger issue has to do with the impact of Church teaching in the area of human sexuality on the human person. How does it impact one's "openness to being," the "realization of every potential within the personality," the "continued discovery and expression of authentic selfhood"? Suggesting that same-sex behavior is "essentially disordered," "objectively grave," and "intrinsically evil" isolates and marginalizes LGBTQ individuals, who are cut off from sexual/romantic relationships. It contributes to division in families, and creates "minority stress," specifically higher prevalence of depression, mood, and/or stress disorders related to the experience of sexual prejudice.

Early in my career, I treated a man who was a member of a religious community. He was depressed and struggling with concerns about his growing awareness of his same-sex orientation. He talked about feeling "different" from other males as early as age three. He came from a very large Catholic family who apparently had some conflict about this issue; his relationship with his father was especially problematic. One of the big issues which he worked to overcome was his belief that he was somehow a "mistake," that God had "made a mistake." My client eventually made the decision to leave his religious community, and he began to explore relationships as a lay person. We worked together for several years. A number of years later, he sought treatment with me again, this time to work through his grief over the loss of his mother. He had found work that seemed challenging and satisfying to him, and he had established a more stable relationship with another man. The outcome of his story was a good one, but the conflict stirred up because of the impact of his strong religious beliefs on his self-image and self-esteem was persistent and very difficult to overcome.

Psychological perspectives/communication

If we look at the conversations between the CDF and the group of Catholic theologians who have provided alternative perspectives on sexual morality, it is apparent that these

conversations reflect very serious problems in communication. To use the terminology of the CDF, we might say
that this communication is "essentially disordered" and that
the problems are "objectively grave." My comments here
are based on the work of Watzlawick, Beavin, and Jackson
(1967) and others who have built on this work in the area
of communication, or "creation of meaning" (Sieburg, 1985,
p. 41). These writers begin with two assumptions: "one cannot *not* communicate" (Watzlawick et al, p. 49). "Activity or
inactivity, words or silence all have message value: they influence others and these others, in turn, cannot *not* respond to
these communications and are thus themselves communi-
cating" (Watzlawick, p. 49). The second assumption is that
each message has two parts, or levels of meaning: the content
of the message, and a relationship aspect. The second level
of meaning, which is a communication about the communication, or a metacommunication, "refers to what sort of
message it is, how it is to be taken, or to the relationship
between the communicants" (Sieburg, p. 58).

In this example, the content of the communication has to
do with sexual morality. In the case of the discourse between
the magisterium and the group of theologians comprising
Curran, Kosnik, McNeill, and others, the response of the
magisterium, first of all, reflects power assertion. The metamessage here is that one is right because one is bigger or
stronger, or somehow in control of the situation. This may
also be viewed as a "disqualifying technique" in that it is an
attempt to invalidate the communication of these scholars by
denying their self-definition, as scholars or experts in the field.
In the case of the social scientists whom I have quoted here,
the metamessage is what would be termed a "disconfirming

response." That is, it goes beyond the rejection implied in the attempts at invalidation and says, in effect, "You do not exist" (Walzlawick, p. 86), i.e. as someone taking part in the conversation. "Disconfirmation, as we find it in pathological communication, is no longer concerned with the truth or falsity ... of P's definition of him/herself, but rather negates the reality of P as the source of such a definition" (Watzlawick, p. 86). These disqualifying and disconfirming responses are characteristic of some of the pathological communication patterns found in families with a schizophrenic member. Some theorists (e.g., Laing, 1959) view the family context as important in creating and/or maintaining, for example, the schizophrenic disorder in an individual.

Tony's deep sense of inclusion, his "round table" ministry, would serve us well in conversations going forward.

God's Holy People

Those friends thou hast, and their adoption tried,
grapple them unto thy soul with hoops of steel.
Hamlet, Act 3, William Shakespeare

For Tony, sending out Christmas cards was a longstanding and important tradition. Each year, he would send Christmas cards to more than 250 of his closest friends and family members. First he picked out the cards, including cards for people who were not Christian, or who were not religious. He then went out to buy special Christmas stamps to put on the cards. And he spent hours and hours writing messages and signing each one. He would save up the Christmas cards that he received and read them all on Christmas Eve. After we were married, it was Tony's job to write our Christmas letter. I have always liked his greeting: *Dear Family, Friends, and God's Holy People.* I think it captures something about his understanding of human relationships, his relationships, each of which was special and important.

At the time of his ordination in 1955, Tony made an implicit commitment to celibate chastity, forgoing marriage and other sexual relationships. This formed a backdrop for his subsequent encounters with people. Celibacy is "the

renunciation of marriage and any voluntary sexual pleasures"
(Egan, NCR, May 12, 1995). It "involves an honest and
sustained attempt to live without direct sexual gratification
in order to serve others productively for a spiritual motive"
(Sipe, 2003). Egan notes that a vow of celibacy "is not made/
taken/given/received." Although this vow was not explicit
during the rite of ordination to the priesthood in 1955, the
expectation was clear. Since Vatican II, candidates for ordination are asked during the rite: "Are you resolved to remain
celibate for the sake of the kingdom and in lifelong service
to God and mankind?"

In the history of the Catholic church, attempts were made
to mandate celibacy for priests, beginning in the fourth century. These were not universally applied until 1022, when
Pope Benedict VIII banned marriages for priests. In 1075,
Pope Gregory VII barred married priests from saying Mass
and from "all ecclesiastical functions." The First Lateran
Council passed an enactment in 1123 which held that marriages by clergy were invalid. The Second Lateran Council
of 1139 endorsed this enactment. It forbade priests to marry
and declared all existing marriages of priests null and void.
During the 1500s, the Council of Trent endorsed the prohibition on married priests and instituted further reforms to
ensure mandatory celibacy.

It has been noted by some writers that economic reasons were important in these mandates for priestly celibacy.
"Legacies for the children of priests [during the 1100s] had
become excessive and the solvency of church properties was
endangered. The most important reason for this reformative
decision was not that celibacy was seen as a higher or purer
state of life, or even that unmarried clerics would be more

free to devote themselves to the care of souls. The chief reason, it appears was economic—not an evil motive, but not a reason intrinsically related to the sacrament of Holy Orders" (Egan, 1995).

Nevertheless, the Catholic church has continued to require celibacy for priests. More recent Church documents reflect this mandate. In 1967, Pope Paul VI issued an encyclical, *Sacerdotalis Caelibatus* (of priestly celibacy), which reaffirmed the Church's stance on celibacy for priests. In 1992, Pope John Paul II issued the following statement: "The Synod does not wish to leave any doubts in the mind of anyone regarding the Church's firm will to maintain the law that demands perpetual and freely chosen celibacy for present and future candidates for priestly ordination in the Latin Rite."

Proponents of celibate chastity have argued that it is "for the sake of the kingdom." This means that the priest is free from family concerns, so that he can be devoted to his ministry. It is also based on the identification of the priest with the person of Jesus, who was presumed to have been celibate throughout his lifetime. And celibacy is viewed as a sign of the kingdom of God, a glimpse of something above, or beyond our earthly existence. It is a discipline, a kind of self-denial. It is not for everyone, but "for those to whom it is given" (Mt 19:11).

In any case, celibacy, with these layers of meaning and history, was important in all of Tony's relationships. In his encounters with people, he was both pastoral and personal, pedagogical and personal, sacramental and personal. "Reciprocity, mutuality, and affection shared with many and not one or an exclusive few become channels which mold and shape priests' pastoral love and their sexuality" (NCCB, *Program of Priestly Formation, 4E.* 1992). There were clear boundaries around genital sexual expression. Tony noted that, early in his priesthood, he wanted to *pull down the shade* over his sexual feelings, as he came to terms with this dimension of his lifestyle. The boundaries around affection, emotional intimacy, and self-disclosure, however, were not so clear. Relationships were complicated, sometimes difficult, because of competing expectations. Tony believed that the values for healthy relationships presented in *Human Sexuality*, which were presumed to foster creativity and integration, applied to persons who made a celibate commitment as for any other person. "The experience of human sexuality within the context of creative fidelity to a covenant commitment must be for the celibate and the virgin what it is for any human person: self-liberating, other-enriching, honest, faithful, socially responsible, life-serving, and joyous. There are signs that such a goal can be achieved" (Kosnik et al., 1977, p. 186).

My own work as a clinical psychologist is all about relationships. In my practice of psychotherapy, my encounter with each client is genuine, honest, and personal, but directed at the client's emotional needs. I try to be present to each client, in each psychotherapy session. I work to create a safe space in which we are able to examine the expectations and ways of relating that each person brings. The boundaries are very clear, and my personal life is separate. These are real and important relationships, but they are not friendships, not romantic relationships. There are boundaries around touch, around self-disclosure of the therapist, which have the purpose of protecting what I have come to understand as a very sacred kind of relationship. Which is to say that I appreciate the complexity and the challenges of the commitment to celibate chastity.

Tony was kind, respectful, faithful, and often joyous in his relationships with others. Many were drawn to him. He allowed people to inhabit his life, to pitch their tent and set up camp if they needed to. Some stayed longer than others. Some never left. The notion of family, and the value placed on family, were deeply engrained in Tony's person, his life, his ministry, and in his understanding and experience of all of these relationships. Wherever he went, Tony made family.

In the Kosnik (Laskowski)/Gorzenski (Jablonski) family, Tony was the great connector. Everyone from the closest to the farthest reaches of this large extended family knew Father Tony. He presided at countless baptisms, weddings, funerals, and family gatherings. He organized overseas trips to make connections with family in Poland and Germany. Father Tony was the one who kept the family together. My son, who is an only child, has always been impressed that there is family everywhere you go. And they feed you and take you in when you go there. He was especially moved by this during two business trips to Germany. Some of Tony's German cousins organized a small family reunion for him while he was there.

In an earlier chapter, I wrote about Tony's relationship with his friend Stasiu. From their first weeks in the high school boarding school, Stasiu (later Father Stan Kukulski) became Tony's brother. Tony and Stasiu talked and argued (endlessly), worked and played together, and got each other into trouble over the years. They studied and traveled together, played (endless) golf together, were ordained together. They shared everything, although at one point Tony refused to room with Stasiu because of Stasiu's smoking habit. They took each other's family as their own. My sister-in-law, Angie, took her first overseas trip with Tony and Stasiu when she was eighteen, and she helped to take care of Father Stan at the end of his life.

Among his papers, I found a letter that Tony wrote to Tony Ervin, a man whom he had come to view as a "spiritual son" on the occasion of Tony Ervin's sixtieth birthday. Tony had met him as a young adult struggling with significant family tragedies. In the letter he commented on the forty years of their relationship. *Over the [last] forty years we have struggled together with your decision to continue in college, to change a medical degree program for one in engineering, to work through a decision to marry ... to decide on adopting a child, and finally, simply to continue to share your life and new family and friendship with me over the years. ... Without fear that this will go to your head, I can honestly confess that you have been and are one of the most loving, sensitive, caring, faithful, and responsible people I have ever come to know. It has been a real privilege that I am deeply grateful for. And your decision to marry and invite me to witness that celebration and then for both of you to choose to adopt a child and nourish her growth to the beautiful young lady she has become has brought me great joy and a sense of fulfillment I otherwise would have never known.* I think that the letter captures something very important about the quality of his relationships and the meaning they had for him.

After he left the seminary at Orchard Lake, Tony contin-ued teaching at Marygrove College, where he directed the Pastoral Ministry program, and at Ecumenical Theological

Seminary, where he directed the Doctor of Ministry program for ministers from a variety of religious groups. Throughout the course of his ministry, he was also highly respected for his work in medical ethics, and he provided consultation in this area for the Mercy Health System, later Trinity Health, as well as for other groups. Through these various ministries, he developed close friendships with women religious. He supported and validated their work. He celebrated their accomplishments. He said Mass for them, conducted retreats, and developed relationships with their religious communities and with their families. He brought them to his family gatherings.

These are just glimpses. Tony was, in turn, deeply affected by all of the people he encountered. Through them, he came to understand some of the complexities of human interactions. He came to appreciate the struggles of people in their relationships, in experiences of loss, betrayal, abuse. He learned to value the contributions of women, especially in their work in his patriarchal church. After his death, I received cards and letters from many people who wanted to say something about what he meant to them. Overall, they were deeply grateful.

> Tony had been a dear friend in times past ... Tony and I spent only a few years together as we authored that moral theology work that resulted so sadly for Tony. Surely he has welcomed God's embrace.
>
> *William Carroll, co-author of Human Sexuality*

I am one of the group who were fortunate to work with Tony many years ago, when the Catholic Society (Theological) of America mandated a study of human sexuality ... Your dear husband was a gifted, wonderful, beautiful man. Those of us who knew him were blessed and fortunate.

Sister Agnes Cunningham, co-author of Human Sexuality

In his role as priest, Tony challenged us all to be adult Catholics and form consciences by which we could make sound and Gospel-centered decisions. In his role as educator, he expanded his students' ability to think and to be their best selves. In his role as friend, he made us feel welcome and accepted in his presence ... My life was enriched by his friendship.

Bishop Tom Gumbleton

Tony was like a big brother I never had. I've known him since I was ten years old, and he taught me catechism for my Confirmation ... I know he lived a holy life.

Sister Naomi

Thank you for introducing us and suggesting that he sit on my dissertation committee. Reflecting on that time, I recall becoming acutely aware of all the things I "did not know" about God, religion, and faith development. I'm sure Tony knew this, but

his guidance allowed me to be comfortable with
"all I do not know." I grew, matured, and finished
the project under his (and your) guidance. As an
adult, I still struggle with "all I do not know," but
it gets easier with time. I know that Tony fostered
this growth in me. For that, I am forever grateful.

Dr. David Michalec, former doctoral student

In 1982 Uncle Tony officiated my Beth's/my
wedding in San Diego. I admired his humor,
warmth, and courage. I always admired his courage
after writing the book and his determination to
say what he believed, especially when it helped so
many of us Catholics who saw life that same way.

Mark Kosnik, nephew

We both loved Tony. He was a great teacher, friend,
and my last tie to Orchard Lake. He brought the
Church to life with the Council and Cardinal
Dearden. It was alive. His writing and his
friendship so true ... Tony spoke at my First Mass,
guided me when I left in 1983 and helped with
laicization, but the Church has been so harsh and
hard up of late ... I have referred to the education
at Orchard Lake in the 60s—dynamic and alive
and Tony led the pack. I was crushed when he
resigned (?) from Orchard Lake. He said his base
was in Detroit so he stayed. I hope he taught from

the classroom or pen because I know he taught from his life.

Stan Zagraniczny, former seminary student

We really appreciated the time in getting to know Tony as the officiant for Kelly and Richard's wedding. Together, you both delivered such a personal meaningful, and intimate message for their life in their ceremony that will never be forgotten. Again, our family had the pleasure of sharing in the joys of life at Matthew's baptism. It was so important to Kelly and Richard that you and Tony could be a part of this celebration. We delight now in the memory of Tony holding Matthew, as a "family" sharing a great meal together, and toasting to an event that brings us together in our Christianity.

Parents of former doctoral student Dr. Kelly Bryce

And finally, a visual: During the offertory procession at his funeral Mass—where "gifts," that is, bread and wine, are brought to the altar to be blessed and consecrated—Tony's nieces formed a long procession, each carrying a rose for him.

Left: Tony with Stasiu (Rev. Stanley Kukulski), lifelong friends, 1960s.

Right: Tony and Stasiu, on the occasion of a Kosnik family wedding, 2001.

Bottom: Tony with his 'adopted son,' Tony Ervin, 2013.

Top: Smelling the roses. Tony at 3308 Doremus, Hamtramck, in 1993.

Bottom: Friends from Orchard Lake seminary, Bob and Maria Geryk,
on vacation with us at Suttons Bay, Michigan, 2011.

Marriage

I will celebrate your love forever, Yahweh. Age on age, my words proclaim your love. For I know that love is built to last forever. Founded firm, your faithfulness.

(Ps. 89)

I will love you and honor you all the days of my life.

From our marriage vows, May 25, 2002

At the time of our marriage, Tony and I had been friends for twenty years. We had become very close and had also collaborated professionally, teaching and conducting workshops together. One of the first times that we worked together was in 1983, shortly after I had completed my Ph.D. We conducted a workshop on sexuality at the Jesuit novitiate in Berkley, Michigan. In this day-long event, we presented a broad overview of psychological and theological perspectives on human sexuality to a group of seminarians. These were young men contemplating their own commitment to ministry in the Catholic church, which included a commitment to celibate chastity. During one of our breaks, Tony and I took a short walk in the neighborhood, then sat under a tree to eat our lunch. Tony commented that women and men who conducted this kind of workshop together usually ended up getting married. My memory of this moment is that we both thought he was joking and laughed.

We thought we knew a lot about marriage. Perhaps we did. Together and separately, we had extensive teaching experience in the areas of human sexuality and marriage. We had each done academic writing in our respective disciplines in these areas as well. Tony had prepared many couples for marriage, presided at their weddings, and provided pastoral counseling to many who were struggling. In my clinical practice, I treated many couples. At the university, I prepared clinical students for working with couples in therapy. I was also privileged to participate in research on marriage that was part of a much larger project conducted by Drs. Carol and Glenn Weisfeld, whose work was directed at evolutionary and cross-cultural perspectives on marriage. I had been married once before.

Given the high divorce rate, about 50% in the U.S., why does anyone get married? In their writing about motivation for marriage, the Weisfelds describe a "pair bonding motive," or "amorousness," or falling in love, which is thought to maximize reproductive success. They note that marriage is "virtually universal," although the role of cultural values and social experience needs to be addressed in studying marriage. From both evolutionary and object relations theoretical perspectives, "pair bonding" represents a form of attachment behavior, which originates in proximity-seeking behaviors seen in infant-caregiver interactions (Bowlby, 1988). Object relations theorists view attachment as a manifestation of a basic and primary human motivation to seek connection with another human being.

Something very important that I have learned in my work in this area is that couples have their own assumptions and motivations, and that each couple creates their own version of marriage out of their lived experience. Tony wrote a letter to his family and friends announcing and explaining his decision to give up public priestly ministry and enter marriage and sent it out on May 24, 2002, the day before our wedding. *After forty-seven years of priestly ministry and much prayer, reflection and consultation, I have decided to give up my public priestly ministry and enter marriage. The reasons for such a serious decision are many, and I thought it might be helpful to share but a few of my reflections with you.* Tony went on to describe his perspective:

> *I have always believed in the beauty and sacredness of marriage. Probably, a lesson learned firsthand from Mom and Dad. I have often thought of it as God's preferred way of calling most of humanity out of themselves to experience and give witness to the God of love who created us. As John the Apostle puts it: "God is love and whoever lives in love lives in God and God in them" (1 John 4:16). Having witnessed many of your marriages this is the one message I always hoped to communicate. After some twenty years of sharing various experiences of life together, I believe I have found the person with whom our shared life can become a deep experience of God and a sacred sign (sacrament) of God's loving presence in the world.*

My announcement was in the form of a poem that I sent to my writing group, who were meeting the night before our wedding:

Wedding (Mine and Ours)

I am getting married tomorrow
tomorrow
I say it again, pinch myself
make sure I'm not dreaming

I don't remember how to do this.

My sister says
I have to carry flowers
wear a special dress
the rest will be easy

My friend's daughter is a wedding planner
she says buy new underwear at Harp's
(established forty-seven years)
Mrs. Harp says
I don't need a slip
and
congratulations dear

I don't remember how to do this.

Some people say
you're too old why are you doing this now
(we don't tell them
our hearts beat strong and true for each other still
and always)

My mother says
he's a good man
already part of our family a long time
do what makes you happy

I don't remember how to do this.

My son and daughter-in-law say
it's about time
you're good for each other
we love you

I will remember this,
pin it on my sleeve
carry it with my flowers tomorrow.

We had shared our decision with members of our immediate families earlier. In March, we invited two of Tony's
brothers and their wives, Leonard and Irene and Bernie and
Louise, to dinner. Leonard was the eldest, the "patriarch."
Bernie was Tony's closest brother. Tony and Bernie had talked
before this. So we sat at table, and Tony announced that we
planned to marry. There were some (eternal) moments of
silence. Then Leonard said, "What can we do to support
you?" There were brief rumblings in the Kosnik family after
this. Someone said, "Let's try to talk Tony out of it." But
Irene said no, and that was the end of it. Overall, our family
and friends provided an outpouring of love and support for
our decision. Two of my friends wrote poems, reflecting on
the deeper understanding of togetherness in "old love," and
on the experience of "standing together as one."

But I'm not sure that any of this captures the complexity
of our "decision story." We had talked about marriage over
the years. It was a difficult question. Tony's commitment to
ministry was a primary consideration for him, and for me
in support of him and his sense of who he was. In his ministerial role, he was also part of a culture. This was a clerical
culture, as well as a culture of religious life. One was called
by God to enter this life. There were rules, expectations, and
loyalties connected to this life and to those who shared it.
Tony wasn't particularly invested in the status of his role. He
had been sent to Rome to study as a young priest, in preparation to become a bishop. The response of the magisterium
to *Human Sexuality: New Directions in American Catholic
Thought* in the 1980s, however, put an end to this career
path. What his role did provide was "standing." He had a
voice that carried some authority, and he was able to use that

for good, in support of the people whom he served. He was deeply committed to his ministry, his teaching, writing, pastoral work, and sacramental ministry. Leaving public priestly ministry for marriage would significantly affect this work. It might also be experienced as a kind of betrayal by his friends who were not willing to leave the priesthood or religious life. His closest friend, Stasiu, was a priest forever.

The available solutions were not very satisfying. Some priests had talked about and opted for a "third way," staying in active ministry and having a partner as well, who would be hidden. I have a friend, Elinor, who loved a priest and consented to this arrangement. She stayed with him for some years until his death from cancer. In the months prior to his death, he was somehow permitted to live in her home. His "brother priests" would come to visit. One of them said to her, "I have an Elinor, and her name is Patricia." Her name is Sarah, Jean, Aileen, Evelyn, Judy, Mary Lou, Paula, Colleen, Mary, Irma, Javan, Mary Sue, Kay, Madelyn, Marie, Patty. Her name is Every Woman who has given up her life for this kind of love.

There were consequences for me as well. I would not be available for another romantic relationship. I would not be able to have more children. I would have no clear role in Tony's life. At best, I would be invisible. At worst, I would be seen as a caricature, a foolish woman chasing a man who was not available, Tony's "girlfriend." What would this mean for my professional identity? How could I be authentic with my family and friends if I could not speak about the most important relationship in my life? This version of me did not jibe with Tony's experience of me or of our relationship.

Most of you know Peggy Stack. We have been friends for over twenty years now. She was one of the first in the early 1980s to write a strong letter of support on my behalf to Cardinal Szoka when my ouster from Orchard Lake was being contemplated. We have been partners in a prayer group, conducted workshops together, taught together, shared family parties and gatherings and supported one another through these years. She is a Diplomate Doctor of Psychology on the Faculty of the University of Detroit-Mercy and Director of their Psychology Clinic. More than that, she is a gourmet cook, a great seamstress, a wonderful homemaker, a sensitive, creative, thoughtful, faith-filled, and fun-loving person to have as a partner for life. She also paints, plasters, does plumbing and tiling like an expert. And besides, I love her.

And what about love? What is passionate love? The Weisfelds (2018) talk about hormonal levels. "Amorousness and other social bonds are related to levels of oxytocin and vasopressin. In humans, brain areas with vasopressin and oxytocin receptors are involved in pair bonding and maternal care" (p. 9). Leonard Cohen has a different take on the experience in his "Hallelujah." "I remember when I moved in you. The holy dove, she was moving too. And every breath that we drew was hallelujah." In the Song of Songs, from the Hebrew scriptures, the lovers speak: "I am my Beloved's and his desire is for me ... Set me like a seal on your heart, like a seal on your arm. For love is strong as Death ... Love no flood can quench, no torrents drown" (7:11, 8:6). Other writers will say that this experience of love is brief, fleeting. I am not so sure of that. At the end of Tony's life, as I bathed and dressed him, I thought that these touches were of a piece with our passionate love. In the movie Shadowlands, which tells the story of the relationship between C. S. Lewis and American poet Joy Davidman, and her death from cancer, there is a scene in which Joy tells Lewis that it is all one, the joy of their love, her cancer, and eventual death. I think of it like that.

Eventually, we sought out consultation from friends, a couple who were credentialed and active in the field of ethics. They talked us through the ethical implications of our decision, for ourselves, each other, our work, and our relationships with family and friends. This conversation provided a turning point for us. We began to plan for our life together and were married a year later. Some years before, I had treated a priest who ultimately left active ministry to marry. He talked about his decision to leave the priesthood. He said that deciding to leave was like facing a rushing river, and that when he made the decision and looked back, he could see that it was a little stream. Tony was eloquent on this point. In his letter to family and friends announcing his leaving and our marriage, he wrote:

> Now for my decision to leave the priesthood. Ever since Vatican II, i.e. for over thirty years, I have questioned, wondered, spoken, and written challenging the wisdom of much church teaching in the area of sexuality. I remain convinced that in spite of the church's dismissal of my major effort "Human Sexuality: New Directions in American Catholic Thought" the views expressed there are closer to God's

truth and the convictions of God's people than current Church teaching. Survey after survey indicate that the majority of conscientious Catholics do not accept Church teaching on masturbation, birth control, contraception, sterilization, artificial insemination, stem cell research, divorce-remarriage-annulment practice, homosexuality, and of course, most recently, mandatory celibacy. In addition to these issues, the authoritarianism in the Church that discriminates against women, forbids inclusive language in the liturgy, prevents National Conferences of Bishops from addressing meaningfully their own regional issues (The Pastoral On Women, the Mandatum for Theology Teachers, Liturgical Language, etc.), narrowly restricts episcopal nominees, and suspends or excommunicates its best theologians without due process, is not a Church leadership that reflects the vision Christ came to give us.

The harmful effects of these church teachings and policies for individuals and the church as a whole has become over the years ever more evident. For years I have been encouraging people to follow their well-formed conscience, even when it goes against church teaching. I have been repeatedly disappointed by bishops and priests who refuse to speak out openly and work for change when they no longer believe in church policy. Not to follow my own convictions in this matter would add to the scandal that is destroying the church and betray my own integrity and all that I have tried to teach others.

Tony did not regret his years of ministry, and he continued to value his Church.

> *I have always treasured my priestly ministry and am deeply grateful for the many opportunities it offered for personal enrichment and service to others. I have no regrets for the many years of that life. I will certainly miss the opportunities it offered and regret the disappointment and loss my leaving may cause. The recent revelations about priestly misconduct convince me all the more that the church's policy of mandatory celibacy is not a blessing. That policy contributes to the diminishing number of priests, to the closing and consolidating of our parishes, to the deprivation of our people of the sacraments and pastoral services so badly needed to carry out the mission of Christ. When I made my commitment to celibacy, I was convinced that though it was a great personal sacrifice, it was one that made sense in the light of that goal. Today, I believe that mandatory celibacy is a serious obstacle to that mission. I no longer find the reasons to remain celibate convincing and hope that my action will be understood not as an abandonment of my faith but a living out of my conscientious convictions. Although I will no longer exercise my priesthood publicly, I hope in every way possible to continue living out my Catholic faith, serving God's people and building the kingdom of God.*
>
> *Although the official church disciplined me and treated me like an unwanted step-child and an*

> *embarrassment to it, I must confess that many of the faithful whom I served were much more understanding and supportive. With the Vatican's recent declaration that dissent from the Church's moral teaching is largely responsible for the recent scandals, I fear that I would only become an even greater embarrassment and more vocal critic of the church. Neither of us need that now.*

What I have come to understand about Tony's decision to leave active ministry and to marry is that it represented an act of courage. He left the life that he knew and entered something wholly other. It is one thing to study, to talk about marriage, to provide counsel for those struggling with marriage, and another to live it. To do that at seventy-one, after forty-seven years of priesthood, was something. It was challenging for both of us. I was not always patient with his friends and their expectations, and he did not always understand my boundaries. I think that our tenacity, Tony's kindness, and perhaps my cooking, helped us to hold on. Our commitment certainly deepened over the fifteen years of our marriage. As stated in an earlier chapter, when my two grandchildren (then six and ten) needed to come and live with us, Tony took them in without question, provided for them, cared for them as his own. And they stayed until and beyond his death. His commitment to them did not waver. In 2014, we went to Mass with our friends who were celebrating their fiftieth wedding anniversary. They were going to renew their vows. The priest who was celebrating this Mass invited all the married couples to come up and renew their vows. So we did. This was a very profound experience for both of us. In that moment, I had a deep sense that what we were doing together was right and good, that our marriage was generative. Tony would call it a *sacred sign*.

On the occasion of our wedding, May 25, 2002, with Rev. Ray and Linda Babin. Ray officiated the ceremony.

Marriage vows, Tony and Peggy, May 25, 2002.

11

Sensus Fidelium

Looking back over the years of our marriage, it is clear to me that Tony never gave up his priestly ministry. This way of being in the world, and his convictions about what was really important, were so deeply held, that he could not give it up. But something had shifted in him after our marriage. He began to identify as one of "God's holy people," not as one apart. This new identity profoundly affected his thinking and the character of his ministry. This was evident as he faced dementia and other age-related diminishment at the end of his life. He bore witness to these experiences, rather than retreat into hopelessness. Although, I know that he suffered.

My mother died in 2020, at ninety. She was a fiercely independent woman who had survived many losses. She did not take well to diminishment. It was painful to watch her struggle, and our efforts to help were rejected more often than not. She fell more than once and did not tell us how badly she had been injured. And she insisted on driving when that was not a good choice for her. But at some point in the last months before her death, she told me that it helped her to think of Tony going through this experience the way that he did. Thinking of him with his walker, or transport chair, and all that represented, seemed to make a difference for her.

Tony had some good years before diminishment. He gave several formal talks during the time between 2010 and 2015. He left two papers, prepared for these talks, which provide glimpses into the way he pulled it all together while his thinking was still clear.

The first of these papers is a reflection on the relationship between theology and ideology, prepared for the Wranglers, described in an earlier chapter. In this paper, Tony tried to contrast and compare the two constructs, defining theology as "the study of God and God's relation to the world," and ideology as "a somewhat rigid, inflexible and uncompromising position," or "an obsessive attachment to a single principle that tends to exclude other relevant considerations in its decision-making process." His question: "When does a theological position become ideology, and what is it that makes it so?" He went on to talk about several positions from the Catholic tradition in the field of ethics, which "appear to be more ideological than theological:" birth control, same-sex relationships, and the Church's response to the sex abuse crisis.

Tony's introduction to this talk was revealing. In it he acknowledged the impact of his personal experience on his thinking and his choices, albeit tongue in cheek. *I want to apologize for not having attended many of the sessions of this group. I'm sure it would have enriched my own paper immensely. But my cardiac arrest last July and the subsequent prolonged recovery with no driving privileges made it difficult to get around. I was sure that I was going to be here last month, but my theological argument lost out to my wife's ideological conviction of how we should spend her spring break this year. It goes to prove that theology is not always the better choice.*

Tony went on to answer his question about when a theological position becomes ideology and what makes it so. In his reflections on what he viewed as "theology supplanted by ideology" with regard to birth control, he pointed to the notion of papal infallibility and the "fear of what would happen to church authority if the Pope decided to change a position that was proposed as infallible by a number of Popes over the years." He viewed literal interpretation of Scripture as "the most compelling argument" used to categorize homosexual acts as "intrinsically disordered." "If God has so spoken, who can dare to challenge it?" With regard to the sex abuse crisis in the Catholic church, Tony presented the "sin of clericalism," safeguarding the reputation of clergy at all costs, as blindsiding the Church "to the enormity of the crimes that were being committed" by priests against children.

But how does one "move ... from an ideological to a more open and embracing theological perspective"? Tony noted here that being open to dialogue "can stretch your mind, but dialogue alone is not enough." He closed this talk with a personal example:

> *Let me share my personal experience on that kind of change in my own life. I remember in the seminary objecting to the Church's teaching on birth control. Margaret Sanger was the rage at*

that time. Her argument against natural law was: If you can cut your hair or shave your beard, isn't that against natural law? That to me sounded like a good argument. I don't think my professors ever convinced me otherwise. I heard confessions where birth control was confessed, but I never really believed that sin was being forgiven.

The teaching on homosexuality was quite different. Not being gay myself, I recognized that this is not what I felt and carrying it out universally would certainly end the world as we know it. The Bible I thought spoke clearly about the issue, and the Church taught this for centuries. Who was I to object? For the first ten years of my priesthood, I certainly believed and defended that teaching. In the confessional, I tried to be compassionate and understanding, but in no way did I consider it acceptable behavior. I began writing a column for the Michigan Catholic entitled "Here's the Answer." On the staff was another columnist, a young man [who] wrote a column for teenagers. He was every mother's dream for a son-in-law for her daughter. He was young, intelligent, good looking, and well-connected. His father was on the board of General Motors. We had become very good friends over the years. He asked me one day to go out to lunch ... and during our conversation, he acknowledged his gayness and let me know he was going to come out the following week. He knew it would embarrass his family and probably cost his job. But honesty compelled him to make this choice.

I left that lunch shaken like I had never been in my life. It began a process of rethinking, reading, reevaluating everything I believed about homosexuality. My friend, Brian McNaught, did lose his job and went on to become the founder of the national Catholic organization for gays and lesbians, Dignity. It was a traumatic experience for me but one that brought about a genuine conversion as I tried to reconcile what the Church was saying about this individual and what my personal experience was.

The second paper, *Sensus Fidelium*, captures both thinking and context. The term 'Sensus Fidelium' means that "all of the faithful, possessing the Spirit by virtue of baptism ... are gifted by this same Spirit with an instinct for the truth and a corresponding suspicion of error in matters of faith." All of "God's holy people" (including laity and clergy) share in the mission of the Church. He notes that our baptism "implies an equality among all the people of God that comes before any further distinctions between laity and clergy, and it applies to our work in the world and within the church." Tony's vision of church then reflects "collegial ecclesiology," in contrast to "the hierarchical or pyramidical ecclesiology" embraced by the magisterium. The hierarchical position means that church leadership is led and empowered by the Spirit in the way of truth. The role of the laity in this model is to listen, accept, and obey.

The model of collegial ecclesiology sets out different roles. "It was simply assumed that the Spirit was entrusted to every baptized member of the church, and they all had a voice in discerning God's will. The role of leadership was to facilitate the fullest expression of the gifts of the Spirit and keep the community together."

Although Tony alludes to this position in his earlier work, this paper brings it to the fore. Perhaps the experience of our marriage served as another conversion experience for him, in addition to changing the way that he saw himself. At this point in his life, Tony was searching for truth as one of "God's holy people," whose collective wisdom can be relied upon to lead us home.

Spirituality on Tap: With the Rev. Anthony Kosnik. How should present and future Catholics look at original sin, redemption, salvation and incarnation? 6:30 p.m. March 5, El Sombrero Mexican Restaurant, 8601 Old Thirteen Mile at Chicago Road, Warren. Free. 586-274-0590.

Spirituality on Tap, from the *Detroit Free Press*, 2002. This was one in a series of informal conversations, which included 'Human Sexuality: 25 years later' in 2007.

12

Still Life

My sister, Elizabeth Crank, is an artist, a painter, whose artwork graces the cover of this book. Her most favored subjects are things from our childhood: the grand piano, the loveseats next to the fireplace in the living room, the swing in the yard. Sometimes she selects odds and ends, a bowl or vase, my mother's pewter tea set. She "borrows" these objects and arranges them on her kitchen table. Then she paints. Usually there are no human figures in her paintings, but somehow, they are present. Her paintings evoke memories of times and experiences I thought I had forgotten. I have always painted with words, although at some level, my sister and I understand each other. Her paintings flow between her imagination and the world of real objects, and they form a kind of bridge between her imagination and my imagination.

Tony liked to live in the world of real objects, historical events, and logical thinking. For a long time (before me) he was convinced that he did not dream. Tony appreciated my writing and my sister's paintings. But if we went to the movies, he preferred to see a historical drama—with not too many flashbacks. And he did not like fantasy. One year, he took me to see The Hobbit for my birthday. But his enjoyment was in watching me take delight in the film and not in the story itself.

In his attempt to reflect on his own life, as my sister and I have done with paintings, stories, and poems, Tony took pictures of real people, personal historical events. In my search for his writings, I have found files and boxes of photographs. I have also found cameras and old (working) slide projectors. Tony took many of the pictures, but he also collected pictures that had significance for him from others. The files are stored on the computer in all of the places that photos can be stored. There are boxes in the basement, many boxes, of photographs and slides. Buried in the boxes, I found a spiral notebook that lists some of the early slides. There is no comprehensive list. Some of his photos are arranged in albums. These are easier to decipher and date, since they are organized around specific events, Tony's ordination, his parents' fiftieth wedding anniversary, our wedding.

Tony's memories are stored in the files and the boxes. In the boxes there is a photographic record of our life together, and of Tony's long life before we were together, photos of his childhood, studies in Rome, family celebrations, his extensive travels and many traveling companions. The photographs are revealing in a way that he perhaps did not intend, in that they offer a glimpse of meaning and significance in his life. His selection of pictures was deliberate. What was important to him? Who was important? How do I put the pictures in order?

Tony explored questions about his ancestry throughout his adult life. From whom and from where did he
come? Propped up on his workbench in our basement,
among the hammers, screwdrivers, pipe wrenches, boxes of
screws, electrical tape, and other assorted building materi-
als, is a large photograph of his paternal great-grandfather,
Szymon Kosnik. In the photograph, Szymon is sitting on an
upturned washbasin in a wooded area, somewhere on his
farm in Fisherville, Michigan, near Bay City. He is holding
a large rosary. Szymon was born in the 1830s near Starogard
Gdański, Poland. He emigrated to the U.S. in 1879. Syzmon's
eldest son, John, Tony's grandfather, was born in Poland on
May 1, 1860. The family story is that John left Poland and
came to the U.S. sometime before his eighteenth birthday
to escape conscription into the Prussian army. It appears
that his father Szymon, mother Julia, and younger brother
Thomas followed. After coming to the U.S., Szymon was
able to obtain a land grant in the Fisherville area and settled
there with his family. In the picture, Szymon looks content,
peaceful. He belongs in this place.

Tony made many trips to Poland during his adult life,
to gather as much information as he could find about his
family origins, through records that could be found. He
collected family photographs from the late nineteenth
century, some from Poland, many from the U.S., beginning
with Szymon, and through his own childhood in the 1930s
and 40s. There are formal family portraits, rows and rows
of Kosniks, Gorzenskis, Laskowskas, Jablonskis, posed and
dressed up for the occasion, serious, determined, unsmil-
ing, except for the small children. These were large families,
Catholic, Polish-speaking. The men were farmers, workers

in the building trades, and factory workers, hard-working, ready for new life in America. The women worked at home managing the care and feeding of their families, birthing many children who grew up to be engineers, lawyers, doctors, teachers, businesspeople, and in the Kosnik-Gorzenski family, two priests.

Tony's Polish Catholic roots are well-represented in his collection of photographs. Tony struggled to understand his Polish origins as he found himself at odds with a Polish pope, John Paul II, over the publication of *Human Sexuality*. We traveled to Poland in 2005, rented a car, and drove from Zakopane on the Czech border in the south to Krakow, Warsaw, Gdansk, Poznan, and points in between. We saw, and Tony photographed, many sites where homage was also paid to John Paul II on signs, posters, dedications to monuments, because of his role in promoting the ideals of the Solidarity movement of the 1980s. It seemed like everywhere we turned, there was another likeness of this Polish pope, another remembrance. One of the sites that we visited was the residence of the Bishop of Krakow, Karol Wojtyla, before he became pope in 1978. Tony had been Wojtyla's houseguest in Krakow with a group attending a theological conference sometime in the 1970s. He noted that he had been concerned at that time about Wojtyla's more authoritarian stance, lack of flexibility in his thinking, *his emphasis on certainty in faith and morals*. But to understand Karol Wojtyla and his thinking meant understanding Polish history, particularly its changing borders over the centuries, and the significance of the Polish Catholic church in preserving Polish identity and culture through all of the changes.

Polish Catholicism is remarkable for the consistency and certainty with which it proclaims official church teachings on faith and morals. It has experienced none of the theological tension, opposition, resistance, and dissent, especially in the area of morals, that has marked western European and American Catholicism in recent decades. In this regard, Polish theological development has been considerably less innovative and more reserved than trends found elsewhere in the world ... The church's struggle for survival against a regime thoroughly committed to its extinction is perhaps the best explanation for this need for absolute clarity and certitude. Our American experience has taught us how disturbing even insignificant changes can be; for the Polish church such divisiveness in their circumstances would have been fatal (p. 26, *The Church In Anguish*, 1987).

In Polish history, there are strong elements of defiance and resistance, which seem contradictory to clarity and certitude, but are somehow of a piece with those elements. Even Wojtyla talked about attitudes of "solidarity" and "opposition" as necessary to each other and natural consequences of communal life and activity (Modras, unpublished manuscript). It appears that Wojtyla was unable to reconcile these attitudes, however, in his responses to theologians such as Tony who attempted critique of the Magisterium. Church authority in Poland reflected this conflict. Tony had a priest friend who was "sent" to a village in the area near Zakopane, after he displeased his bishop. A large proportion of the individuals in this village had a schizophrenic disorder. Tony reported that his friend began his ministry with the members of this faith community by encouraging their efforts at woodcarving. This led to more elaborate artwork. Tony visited his friend during his sabbatical to Poland in 1980. While he was there, he asked one of the artists if he could carve a nativity set for him. They agreed on a price of $20, and Tony gave him $40 to cover the cost of sending it to him. He thought that he was unlikely to see the artwork or his money and chalked it up as a charitable donation. Some months after he returned to the U.S., a large box was delivered to his home in Hamtramck, containing the nativity set and $20. We put up this beautiful piece of Polish folk art every Christmas. During our trip to Poland in 2005, Tony took me to this village. His priest friend had died, but a large building on the church grounds housed an art gallery—rooms and rooms of brightly painted carvings. In one of the rooms, there were other nativity sets like ours. Of course, he took many photos, so we have these as well. For me, this story evokes the imagery of a phoenix rising from the ashes.

Tony's priesthood embodied both solidarity and opposition, perhaps a movement from one attitude to the other. I have described his ordination photos in an earlier chapter. These are carefully ordered in an album, to tell the story of the event, and to explain the significance of each element of the ordination ceremony. This was a very solemn event, reflecting centuries of tradition. For the fiftieth anniversary of Tony's ordination, we held a dinner at our home, inviting all of the members of his class whom we could find. There were thirteen places at the table. As described in an earlier chapter, the party included one active priest, one widow, one widower, and other priests with their wives. We sat at a round table. Such a different model of Church, that included married priests, a round table, both men and women invited to speak.

There is another photograph in Tony's collection that I think provides a link between the two events: Tony's ordination and the fiftieth anniversary celebration. This is a very large black and white photograph of clergy present at the installation of Pope John XXIII, taken with a wide-angle lens. Although it is not in color, it captures the pageantry and ritual of the Church in 1958. There are rows and rows of men in black clerical garb looking toward the center of the Cathedral where the ceremony was taking place, a twenty-eight-year-old Tony in this picture somewhere. John XXIII was a pope who "opened the window" to the kind of change and transformation evident in Tony's anniversary celebration.

Religious celebrations are highlighted in Tony's photos. He witnessed the weddings of most of his own (forty-nine) nieces and nephews, and some of their children, as well as the children of his friends, parishioners, and *God's holy people*. And after the weddings, there were more pictures taken at baptisms and special anniversaries. In the wedding pictures, Tony stands with the brides and grooms during the religious ceremony, and then poses with the new couple. He did a wedding for one of his grandnieces, Megan, in 2009, on the beach of Lake Michigan, the wedding party in formal wear and flip flops, children and families on the beach watching quietly and with great interest. Megan had told him that, since she was a little girl, she wanted him to be the celebrant at her wedding. At his funeral, Megan presented me with a photo of Tony at this wedding, her wedding. In the picture, he is standing on the beach, in his suit and stole, under an arch constructed of sticks and a very long white scarf, waiting for the bride and groom. Tony never saw this picture. But he would remember this moment, and he would have treasured the photograph.

Tony traveled widely, beyond Michigan and beyond the U.S., inviting family members and friends to accompany him. His serious traveling began during the period that he studied in Rome, 1958 to 1961. He used the opportunity to travel as often as he could, through Europe and the Holy Land. In 1980, Tony spent a sabbatical year in Poland, using that as another opportunity to travel further abroad. There were many other trips. The slides from his travels show magnificent sites, as well as glimpses of his traveling companions. Tony's friend, Stasiu, and his sister, Angie, were perhaps the first of a long procession of family members and friends. Tony would assemble a group and then plot out the destinations. He preferred driving trips, so if there was a way to rent a car, he did that. Tony was always a wonderful guide, and he usually was able to speak the language in the countries that he visited. This meant experiencing each place at a deeper and more intimate level. And it was easier to get around and to find whatever was needed—food, lodging, directions, forgotten medications, eyeglass repair. His traveling companions all have stories of the road, as I do.

There are individual photos that stand out for me. One of my favorites is one that was taken in 1960 during a trip to the Holy Land. Tony is riding a camel in Egypt in front of one of the pyramids, wearing a white headpiece. He is smiling in the picture and ready for whatever adventure awaits. He is thirty years old.

Another photo that I treasure was from a trip that we took to Michigan's upper peninsula. We had stopped at the Straits of Mackinac to look at the water. I took this picture of Tony looking at me. There are songs written about that look. My father used to sing them. *Smoke Gets In Your Eyes. The Look of Love. Love Me Tenderly. I Only Have Eyes For You.* I was Tony's last traveling companion. We traveled through the U.S., went to Ireland and England, France, Germany, Italy, Hungary, the Czech Republic, Austria, Spain, and Portugal. We navigated our marriage for fifteen years. With the help of Marilyn, Bobbie, Paul, the "old people," my grandchildren, Sister Jean, and the hospice team, I walked with Tony through his dementia and diminishment to the end of his life at eighty-seven years old. As I am writing this, I realize that he managed to assemble a group for this last trip. I hope that he is having a grand adventure.

Tony's great-grandfather, Szymon Kosnik, who emigrated from Poland in 1879, praying the rosary, Fisherville, Michigan, 1880s.

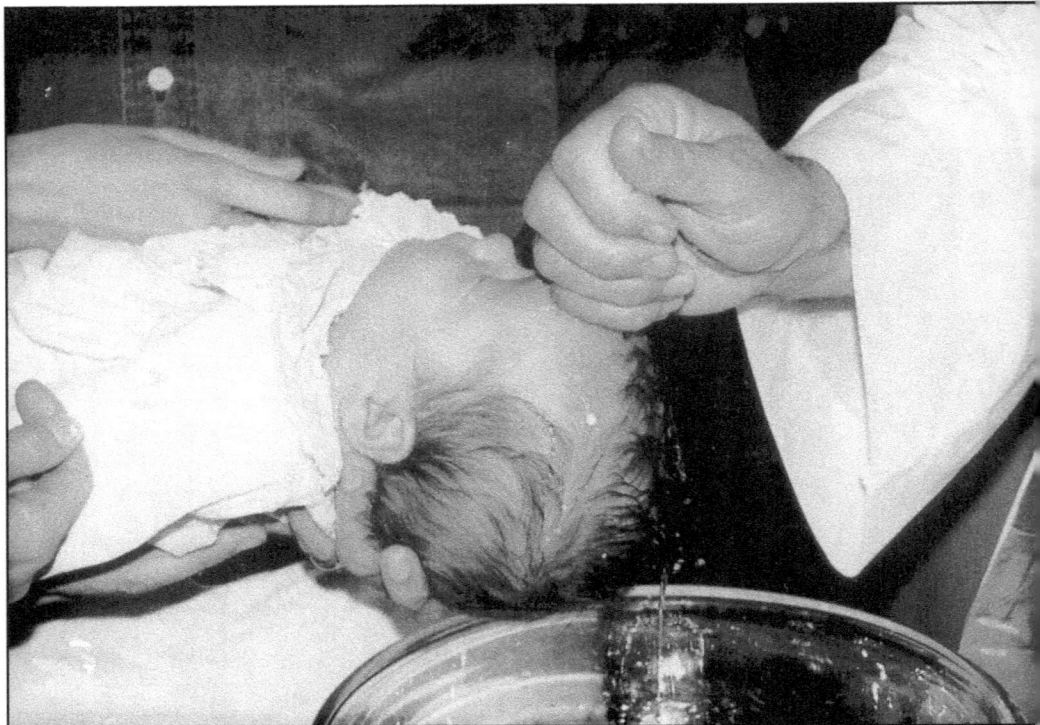

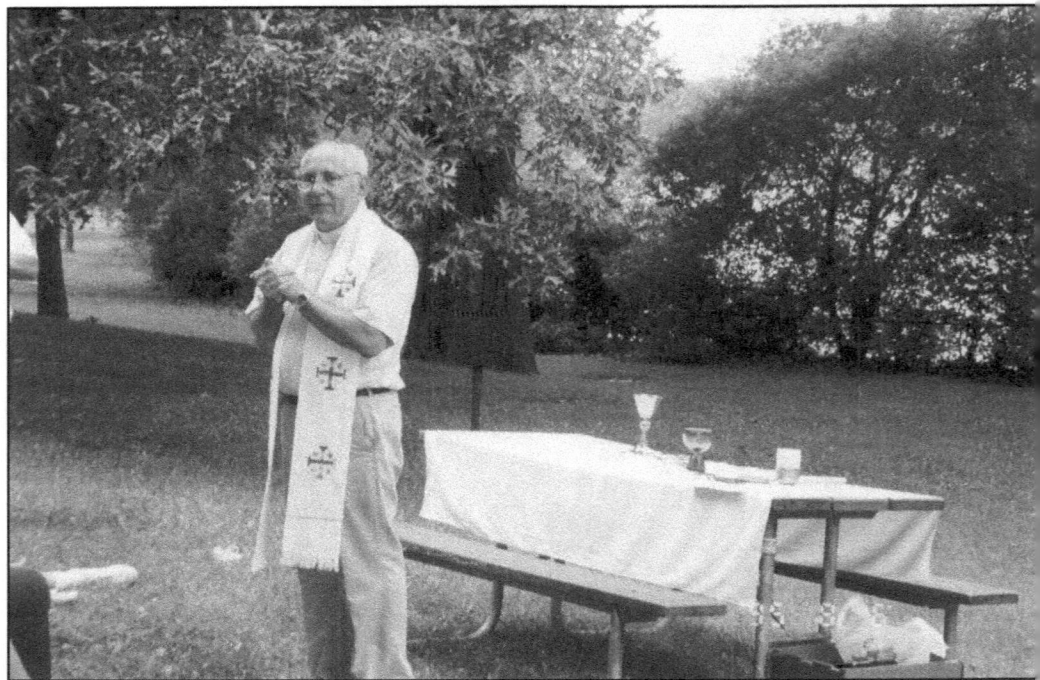

Top: Tony administering the sacrament of baptism, 1998.

Bottom: Tony saying Mass at a family reunion in 1995.

Top: Tony and Peg at Ponte Vecchio, Florence in 2008.

Bottom: Tony looking at me, on a vacation in northern Michigan.

Top: Tony as a young priest in Egypt, riding a camel and
wearing a white headpiece, in front of a pyramid.

Bottom: Waiting for the bride and groom, at Glen Haven, Michigan beach, August 2009.

13

Coda

In music, a coda is a passage that brings a piece to an end.
Technically, it is an expanded cadence. It may be as simple as
a few measures, or as complex as an entire section ... The coda
is often more technically difficult than the rest of the piece.

In examining someone's life, careful listening is called for. The imagery of a piece of music captures something about the process that is important: Listen to the chord progression, the phrasing, new or repeated themes. In my work as a clinical psychologist, conducting a psychological evaluation demands this kind of listening. I tell my students that after collecting the evaluation data from interviews, test results, other records, and clinical impressions, the task is to integrate the information coming from these multiple and different sources to make sense of the whole person. Even then, the process is elusive. The sources contradict one another. Or there is a compelling movement that can lead to an erroneous conclusion if all of the data are not considered. And there is the filter of one's own lens to consider, not to disregard but to use as yet another path to understanding.

My observations in this book are informed by my training and experience as a clinical psychologist. I have drawn on psychological theories and research as pathways to understanding this material. My observations are not distanced or entirely abstract, however. I was Tony's wife, his intimate partner, his last traveling companion. I love(d) him, and this also enhances my understanding.

As I have noted earlier in this work, the task I have undertaken is to pull together pieces collected from Tony's life, to provide some understanding of how he was formed, in and through his family, his relationships, his formal and informal educational experiences, and his church. These are not so separate. At this point I am going to review what I consider to be the major themes, influences, and pathways to his becoming the person he was, who came to think the way that he did and, finally, to say what he had to say. These include his very large family, his Polish ancestry, his Roman Catholicism, his theological training/approach to learning, and what he would name as the Spirit. The quality of his relationships, "the company that I keep," is an underlying and repeated movement that propels him to the next level, and allows for each moment of transformation.

While I did not have an opportunity to observe this directly, the available evidence suggests that Tony formed a secure and positive emotional attachment with his parents. Bowlby (2008) describes the notion of the "secure base" provided by parents, from which "a child ... can make sorties into the outside world and to which s/he can return, knowing that: s/he will be welcomed, nourished physically and emotionally, comforted if distressed, reassured if frightened" (p. 11). The role of the parent is to be available and ready to respond when called upon, to encourage and perhaps assist, but to intervene only when clearly necessary. Attachment theory, as presented by Bowlby and other theorists (Mahler, 2018;

Hazen & Shaver, 1994; Ainsworth, 1978; Fonagy, 1999; Main, 1996) is based on the assumption that the propensity to develop intimate emotional bonds is a basic component of human nature, and that this capacity provides a foundation for effective personality functioning and mental health. There appears to be some kind of independent autonomous need for relationship. A secure and positive bond allows one to explore the world and to develop positive emotional bonds with others. Erikson describes the phenomenon as the achievement of "basic trust" in the world, i.e. development of the belief that one's needs will be met, even in the face of adversity and challenge. Erikson's notion of basic trust has been described as a foundation for religious belief (Rizzuto, 1979).

The "available evidence" of secure attachment for Tony is suggested first in his ability to leave home at a very young age, and to thrive. The evidence also includes his positive and enduring relationships with his parents, as well as his hopeful outlook and openness to experience that persisted throughout his life. With regard to the latter, Tony would talk about his *God of surprises,* which allowed him to consider other possibilities in the face of the unexpected. Based on Tony's descriptions of relationships with both parents, it seems clear that they provided a "secure base" for him. He was able to go out and explore the world at a young age. He was at home in the world. He was able to explore places, and then people and ideas. He went skiing in the Alps. He showed genuine interest in the people whom he met from all walks of life. He was not afraid to think.

Tony's large Polish Catholic family was an important anchor and provided context for his experience of the world.

There was a value placed on family and family relationships, which fostered loyalty and support. Tony tried to create family wherever he went, and with whomever he found himself. Although he was ultimately able to rise above this experience, his sense of betrayal by some of his colleagues at the seminary, as well as by Church authority, when he was forced to leave his teaching position after the publication of *Human Sexuality*, was profound because of the kind of relationships that he had established. The value that Tony placed on family later manifested as a strong sense of social responsibility. Catholic social justice teaching was a recurrent theme in his teaching, especially later in his life. Talks With Tony (Our Lady of the Rosary Parish), Catholics for the Common Good, and Elephants in the Living Room were some of the groups that sponsored him.

In the Gorzenski/Kosnik family there was (and is) a reverence, respect, and appreciation for Anastazy and Angeline. Ultimately, Tony respected the authority of his parents over Church authority when the two collided. This was evident early in his life when he chose to work on a construction project at a Baptist church at the request of his father, in the face of Church teaching that this constituted mortal sin. And it was still clear at the end of his life when he told me, *My mother said that I can't be left alone anymore.* In the context of his life as a priest, this was a revolutionary statement. I wonder now as I am reflecting on these words, if Angeline whispered to him as he was leaving active ministry to marry me.

This family was Polish. There is something about the role of the Catholic Church in protecting Polish culture and identity as the borders of Poland changed over the centuries, that suggests a metaphor for Tony. The borders of his experience changed dramatically as he moved from family to seminary training, to his various travels, roles, and widening circle of relationships, but his Polish Catholic culture and identity remained intact. In talking about his Catholic identity, he would say, *Ain't I a Catholic?* paraphrasing Sojourner Truth's quote and the spirit of what she said, "Ain't I a Woman?" And like his ancestors, he was stubborn and determined. His work ethic was strong.

Solidarity has been an important theme in Polish culture. Tony wrote about this in his chapter on Pope John Paul II (Kung, 1987). *Solidarity is a word which has taken on new life and new meaning in the light of events occurring in Poland in the early 1980s. Lech Walesa's efforts that brought about the swift and massive unionization of the majority of the industrial and agricultural laborers in Poland created a power that, temporarily at least, incapacitated the Polish government and military. ... [Solidarity] in its union form was not the first experience of the power in community togetherness that the Poles had experienced* (p. 28). In this chapter, Tony goes on to quote Cardinal Wojtyla (later John Paul II), who talked about solidarity and opposition in the context of the Solidarity movement. *In fact, he (Wojtyla) insists that genuine solidarity requires a healthy opposition and that both are essential for constructing a strong society. He waxes eloquently when he states that "the structure of community must not only allow the emergence of opposition, give it the opportunity to express itself, but also must make it possible for the opposition to function for the good of the community"* (p. 29). For Tony, these attitudes, of solidarity and opposition, were ingrained.

As was his Roman Catholicism. "Polak, to Katolik"—"To be Polish is to be Catholic."

At the heart of Roman Catholicism are notions of incarnation, redemptive suffering, and resurrection. God is thought to have entered into human experience in the person of Jesus, who was eventually executed by the Romans. Jesus' suffering and death through crucifixion are believed to be a source of redemption for wrongdoing (social sin) and new life. Tony's belief in this tradition meant loving God and neighbor, as well as speaking truth to power in response to injustice. Tony had a strong moral sense, and this got him into trouble, the "good trouble" described by the late Congressman John Lewis. He was forever speaking up through his writing, or by carrying signs and marching, when he perceived injustice or wrongdoing. Tony was particularly frustrated when his peers, bishops and clergy, did not or would not speak up. Or when they betrayed *God's holy people* through abuse of power, or sexual abuse. I still have signs in the garage from a protest that was staged at a local parish in response to an attempt by the pastor to dictate voting. Echoes of Anastazy on strike at Chrysler in the 1930s.

For many years, we walked "The Way of the Cross" on Good Friday afternoon, orchestrated by the Detroit peace community, members of the group taking turns carrying a large cross. This event involved a series of reflections at sites in the city: the old train station, casinos, the Detroit River, the Federal building, and others. These "stations of the cross," each represented in some way the suffering of Jesus, attributed to social sin. There was praying and singing at each station. I can still hear the refrain, *Were you there when they crucified my Lord? ... Sometimes it causes me to tremble,*

tremble, tremble. Tony's sense of the sacred was pervasive. "A guest in the house is God in the house." There was always room for another place at the table. People invited Tony to witness their celebrations, as well as their personal trauma and suffering. He was deeply moved by all of this. I believe that his decision to leave active ministry was motivated, in part, by a desire to enter more fully into the experience of *God's holy people* and their collective wisdom.

Drawing on multiple sources, including dialogue with others, characterized Tony's approach to learning and writing. Ideas were challenged, refined as they were discussed. An important example of this approach in Tony's work was described in an earlier chapter by one of the co-authors of *Human Sexuality,* Bill Carroll: Over the period 1972 to 1976, members of the committee "exchanged papers on the various subjects and then met ... to exchange views, critique, and sharpen our focus. At these meetings, members would bring along relevant ideas and writings of other theologians and members of the CTSA they had come across, or specific issues members of the society wished addressed." All commented on the outside suggestions and concerns. This is an example of many other instances of such collaboration. Tony's later work in administration and teaching in the Pastoral Ministry program at Marygrove College and the Doctor of Ministry program at Ecumenical Theological Seminary, as well as his work with groups like Elephants in the Living Room and Catholics for the Common Good, reflected this kind of process.

This is an important process from the perspective of developmental psychology in that it allows for the development of post-formal thought, characteristic of many adults in

middle to late adulthood. This kind of thinking is viewed as
the next stage of intellectual development following development of the capacity for abstract (logical) reasoning. It is
characterized by the ability to integrate abstract reasoning
with real life considerations, tolerance of contradictions and
ambiguity, awareness of paradox, and awareness of the self
as part of a process, i.e. thinking, that is inherently social. It
is reflective, pragmatic, and flexible in problem solving. For
the post-formal mature thinker, the integration of cognitive
and emotional aspects of experience leads to better coping
and adaptive functioning, or positive adjustment (Labouvie-
Vief, 1990).

Tony's learning style was enhanced by his theological
training. As discussed in an earlier chapter, he described his
approach to the discipline of theology as "inductive" and
listed the following sources of knowledge: Scripture/sacred
writings, tradition, science/reason, experience, and the Spirit.
In this approach, experience is examined in light of the
sources. Experience was Tony's starting point for reflection
and study. His doctoral dissertation, *The Imputability of Acts
of Masturbation Among Males*, would appear to come out
of his experience of adolescent sexuality. *Human Sexuality*
came out of his experience as a priest and confessor. *Fortress
Catholicism: Wojtyla's Polish Roots* (Kung, 1987) represents
a careful examination of the thinking of Pope John Paul II,
whose response to Tony's work in the area of sexual ethics
was troubling for him. At the end of his life, Tony reflected
on his own dementia. Although it was a daily struggle, I
believe that his reflection gave him some peace at the end.
He was able to let go, trust me to be his caretaker.

This is in contrast to a "deductive" theological approach (described in Chapter 8), in which one applies the sources and draws conclusions from them. Coming from the "deductive" perspective, one asks 'what should my experience be?' in light of the sacred sources. Sacred writings are interpreted literally and are considered to have the truth. Tony ultimately rejected the "deductive" approach as too narrow and limiting as he later rejected the "manuals of moral theology" described by Curran, the lens of "what actions are wrong or sinful in light of Catholic teaching?" He was able to develop his thinking from these absolutes, which he had embraced during his adolescence and early adulthood, to more complex analysis. It appears that Vatican II precipitated this shift in his thinking from the more abstract and intellectually and emotionally distanced approach of his doctoral dissertation to thinking reflected in his later work, perhaps beginning with *Human Sexuality*. In this work, he and his committee embraced a "personalist" perspective. As stated in an earlier chapter, this perspective considers what it means to be a human person and attempts to look at the whole human person, in context.

All of this allowed Tony to speak truth to power, to hold fast to his position (based on multiple voices and sources), to counter harmful Church teaching, rhetoric, and practices, from a position of "loyal dissent" (Curran, 2006), addressing problems with Church teaching on sexuality and problems with Church authority. These represent his most important contributions. Tony presented sexual ethics in terms of a set of values to be upheld, rather than acts to be avoided. What is the meaning of the act? Context? What is being communicated? His process of challenging Church authority, appealing to the Sense of the Faithful (*Sensus Fidelium*), the collective wisdom of *God's holy people*, was perhaps more powerful than his critique. Tony implicitly raised questions about Church authority when he suggested that it is the well-formed individual conscience that must have the last word about individual choices and behavior. His inclusion of women, whom he trained for ministry, and support of Dignity and New Ways Ministry, representing the Catholic LGBT community, helped to give voice to those whom the Church would silence.

As I write this, quarantined in my house for fear of the coronavirus, I can still feel Tony's sense of urgency in calling for Church reform. He would attribute this movement to the Spirit, experienced as a voice coming from within. *Prepare ye the way of the Lord.* And then I would like to sing it again for him. Louder. Amen.

Tony with his mother, Angeline.

Afterword

I met Tony Kosnik only on a few occasions. The first was before the 1977 publication of the book, *Human Sexuality: New Directions in American Catholic Thought*. Tony and Ron Modras, two members of the committee commissioned by the Catholic Theological Society of America to do a study on human sexuality, met with a small group of Catholics who were involved in "gay" ministry, as the ministry was called at the time. More than a dozen of us sat in a circle, on chairs or on the floor, in the parlor of the "Pink Palace" (the house was painted pink) where Brian McNaught, the founder of Dignity/Detroit, lived. Tony and Ron came to listen to our stories, to ask questions, and to share some preliminary thoughts about the manuscript they were working on for the Catholic Theological Society of America.

We were all delighted when the book was finally published. Fr. Bob Nugent and I, who co-founded New Ways Ministry to provide education about homosexuality, used *Human Sexuality* extensively in workshops we conducted across the U.S. I very carefully presented the theological positions outlined in the book. It is interesting that subsequent theological writings about the morality of homosexuality can be located in one of the four broad categories described in *Human Sexuality*: (1) Homosexual acts are intrinsically evil. (2) Homosexual acts are essentially imperfect. (3) Homosexual acts are to be evaluated in terms of their relational significance. (4) Homosexual acts are essentially good and natural.

Now, almost five decades later, I continue to use this theological model each time I speak about Catholic ethical positions on homosexuality. Many times, I am asked for a good book to read on sexual ethics. I never hesitate to always recommend *Human Sexuality: New Directions in American Catholic Thought*. I usually add, "Although the book is old, you won't find a more comprehensive or more readable description of the state of Catholic theology on sexuality."

Copies of *Human Sexuality* can still be found in some rectory libraries. During the 1980s and early 1990s, the conservative press lamented that the book was being used as a text in many seminaries. I was thrilled because seminarians needed to know and discuss current sexual realities. *Human Sexuality* also stimulated discussion among ordinary churchgoing Catholics. This grassroots discussion had an enormous value. People saw that the book's pastoral guidelines made sense; they were being reintroduced to the basic Catholic teaching of forming one's own conscience as a final moral arbiter.

Not surprisingly, the Vatican was not happy with the book, which ultimately led to Tony's censure and forced departure in 1982 from Sts. Cyril and Methodius Seminary in the Archdiocese of Detroit, Michigan. It is interesting that, Joseph Ratzinger, a *peritus* at the Second Vatican Council, wrote at its close in 1965, "Over the pope as expression of

the binding claim of ecclesiastical authority, there stands
one's own conscience, which must be obeyed before all else,
even, if necessary, against the requirement of ecclesiastical
authority." A little less than two decades later, when he was
Prefect of the Congregation for the Doctrine of the Faith,
then Cardinal Ratzinger seems to have forgotten about the
priority of conscience in making moral decisions. He stip-
ulated that Tony renounce any opposition to the Church's
sexual teaching.

At the time, many renowned Catholic theologians, such
as Charles Curran, Richard McCormack, Gregory Baum,
Margaret Farley, and John McNeill, were publishing scholarly articles and books which also critiqued traditional
Catholic sexual ethics. This scholarship appeared not only
in the U.S. but also in Germany, France, Belgium, and even
Italy and Spain. The efforts of these theologians were also
rejected by the Vatican. *Nihil Obstats* (official certifications
that a work is doctrinally sound) were withheld. Jobs were
denied and promotions were forfeited. Or a license to teach
at a Pontifical University was withdrawn. Like Tony, many
theologians who courageously published dissenting views
received sanctions from the Congregation for the Doctrine
of the Faith, often resulting in a total silencing.

Change in Theological Climate

A change in this censorious theological-episcopal climate did not happen until 2010 when the sexual abuse
crisis exploded in Germany. About thirty leading moral
theologians contributed to a book called *Future Horizons
of Catholic Sexual Ethics.* Additional articles appeared in

theological journals. The book and the articles added to growing grassroots ferment, influenced the German bishops to inaugurate a Synodal Path, which is a series of discussions involving bishops and laity about reform in the church. Sexuality is one of the discussion topics of the Synodal Path. The other three topics are the role of women, priestly ordination, and power structures.

But not only in Germany, but also in many parts of Western Europe and South America, there are theological and episcopal voices calling for an openness to change. From the Vatican, there is now an openness to listen to the People of God. Since Pope Francis was elected in 2013, there has been no sanctioning of theologians. In remarks made at a 2017 event celebrating the twenty-fifth anniversary of the publication of the Catechism of the Catholic Church, Pope Francis said, "Doctrine cannot be preserved without allowing it to develop, nor can it be tied to an interpretation that is rigid and immutable without demeaning the working of the Holy Spirit." During a 2019 presentation to theologians in Naples, Pope Francis spoke of a church that was less dogmatic in its theology, more in touch with reality, and participating in a dialogue with cultures and other religions. His successor, Pope Leo XIV, also seems to welcome the opinions of the People of God. The Church that Tony envisaged seems to be taking root.

Tony's Legacy

As I reflect on the life of Tony Kosnik and his tremendous contributions to the Church, I feel pride, gratitude, admiration, and solidarity. I feel pride because of Tony's Polish heritage; I too have Polish ancestry. As all four of my grand-parents were born in Poland, I am third generation Polish American. I can relate to the values of family, to the "hello" and "goodbye" hugs as you enter or leave a home, and to the Polish religious traditions that bound Tony so closely to the people he served.

I am grateful for Tony's courage and honesty. His writings have brought practical, theological guidelines about sexuality to masses of people in the English-speaking world. His lectures helped Catholics to make their own conscience decisions about sexual matters. And I feel deep appreciation for his faithful priestly service, his sacramental ministry, and his pastoral visits that brought comfort to those in need.

I admire this man who continued to lovingly serve the People of God, despite denunciation by religious authorities who should have commended him. I admire him, as I did John Lewis, for getting in "good trouble" as, even toward the end of his life, Tony bore witness to the goodness of a married priesthood.

And I feel a sense of solidarity with Tony because, like him, I faced institutional sanctions. While I have lived to see that rejection lifted, Tony unfortunately did not. He bore that burden valiantly.

Tony's life reminds me of a poetic prayer, called "A Step along the Way," by Bishop Ken Untener, a fellow priest of Tony's in the Detroit Archdiocese. Part of the poem reads:

> We plant the seeds that one day will grow.
>
> We water seeds already planted, knowing that they hold future promise. We lay foundations that will need further development.

We provide yeast that produces far beyond our capabilities.

We cannot do everything, and there is a sense of liberation in realizing that. This enables us to do something, and to do it very well.

It may be incomplete, but it is a beginning, a step along the way, an opportunity for God's grace to enter and do the rest.

We may never see the end results, but that is the difference between the master builder and the worker.

We are workers, not master builders; we are ministers, not messiahs. We are prophets of a future not our own.

Each line of "A Step along the Way" seems to describe Tony's life. He was truly one of our Church's prophets. He planted seeds among the hierarchy and among church-going Catholics that enabled them to rethink the traditional framework about human sexuality. Though not yet fully grown, those seeds have begun to sprout now in the Vatican and among the wider Church. There is now an openness to listen to diverse voices in a synodal fashion. Tony watered the seeds and provided yeast by his faithful allegiance to the institutional church and to the People of God.

Tony was at the beginning of a Catholic sexual revolution. He did not do everything that needs to be done to turn around an institution from encrusted attitudes toward sexuality, nor could he; but the realization and the acceptance of that fact gave him a sense of freedom in doing his part, which he did extremely well. Our faith assures us that God's grace will do the rest.

Tony did not live to see the end results (nor may we), but Tony was a faithful minister. He was not the Messiah. He was a worker, not the Master Builder. Tony Kosnik was truly a prophet of a future not his own.

Jeannine Gramick
Feast of St. John Vianney, Curé d'Ars, August 4, 2025

Recommended for Further Reading

The Language of God: A Scientist Presents Evidence for Belief
Francis Collins
Francis Collins, head of the Human Genome Project, describes his own journey from atheism to agnosticism to faith.

Loyal Dissent: Memoir of a Catholic Theologian
Charles Curran
Charles Curran was a contemporary and a friend of Tony Kosnik. This is an account of his own struggles with the institutional Church. He provides an important and comprehensive understanding of natural law.

Just Love: A Framework for Christian Sexual Ethics
Margaret Farley
Margaret Farley provides a contemporary account of Christian sexual ethics from a justice perspective, using a framework for evaluating relationships that also replicates Kosnik's work.

Body, Sex, and Pleasure: Reconstructing Christian Sexual Ethics

Christine Gudorf

In her reconstruction of Christian sexual ethics, Christine Gudorf provides an affirming view of human sexual relationships. She too gives an important and comprehensive understanding of natural law.

The Psychology of Religion and Coping: Theory, Research, Practice

Kenneth Pargament

Kenneth Pargament is a social scientist who has done extensive research on religious belief and its implications for coping. He explores psychological and theological perspectives as different approaches to understanding the human condition.

The Sexual Person: Toward a Renewed Catholic Anthropology

Todd Salzman and Michael Lawler

These are scientists responding to the social implications of Catholic teaching on sexuality. They provide a comprehensive critique of the classicist and ahistorical interpretation of human nature implied in Church teaching.

The Psychology of Marriage: An Evolutionary and Cross-Cultural View

Carol Weisfeld, Glenn Weisfeld, and Lisa Dillon, Eds.

This book provides an extensive review of research on marriage from a social science perspective.

References

Ainsworth, M. D. S. (1978). The Bowlby-Ainsworth attachment theory. *Behavioral and brain sciences*, *1*(3), 436-438.

Allan, G. (2014). Being unfaithful: His and her affairs. In *The State of Affairs* (pp. 121-140). Routledge.

American Psychiatric Association. (2013). *Diagnostic and Statistical Manual of Mental Disorders: DSM-5*. American Psychiatric Association.

Arifain, S. M. K., Yusof, F., Aziz, S., Suhaini, N., & Suhaini, N. (2021). The influence of social support on marriage satisfaction among working women in Selangor, Negeri Sembilan and Melaka. *International Journal of Academic Research in Business and Social Science*, *11*(2), 587-595.

Bell, A. P., & Weinberg, M. S. (1978). *Homosexualities: A study of diversity among men and women*. Simon & Schuster.

Blanchard, R. (2018). Fraternal birth order, family size, and male homosexuality: Meta-analysis of studies spanning 25 years. *Archives of Sexual Behavior, 47*(1), 1-15.

Bowen, M. (1961). The family as the unit of study and treatment: Workshop, 1959: 1. Family psychotherapy. *American Journal of Orthopsychiatry*, *31*(1), 40.

Bowlby, J. (2008). *A Secure Base: Parent-child attachment and healthy human development*. Basic books.

Campbell, T., & van der Meulen Rodgers, Y. (2023). Conversion therapy, suicidality, and running away: An analysis of transgender youth in the US. *Journal of Health Economics*, *89*, 102750.

Camperio-Ciani, A., Corna, F., & Capiluppi, C. (2004). Evidence for maternally inherited factors favouring male homosexuality and promoting female fecundity. *Proceedings of the Royal Society of London. Series B: Biological Sciences, 271*(1554), 2217-2221.

Coleman, E. (Ed.). (1988). *Integrated identity for gay men and lesbians: Psychotherapeutic approaches for emotional well-being* (Vol. 14, No. 1-2). Routledge.

Collins, F. S. (2006). *The Language of God: A scientist presents evidence for belief* (No. 111). Simon and Schuster.

Congregation for the Doctrine of the Faith. (1975). Declaration on certain questions concerning sexual ethics. In Curran, C. & McCormick, R. (Eds.), *Readings in Moral Theology, No. 8: Dialogue about Catholic sexual teaching* (pp. 375-391). Paulist Press.

Curran, C. (1970). Sexuality and sin: A current appraisal. In Curran, C. & McCormick, R. (Eds.), *Readings in Moral Theology, no. 8: Dialogue about Catholic sexual teaching* (pp. 405-417). Paulist Press.

Curran, C. (1972). *Catholic Moral Theology in Dialogue.* Fides publishers, Inc.

Curran, C. (1988). *Tensions in Moral Theology.* University of Notre Dame Press.

Curran, C. E. (2006). *Loyal Dissent: Memoir of a Catholic Theologian.* Georgetown University Press.

De Koning, E., & Weiss, R. L. (2002). The relational humor inventory: Functions of humor in close relationships. *American Journal of Family Therapy, 30*(1), 1-18.

De Roo, R. J. (2012). *Remi De Roo: Chronicles of a Vatican II Bishop*. Novalis.

Dillon, L. M., Nowak, N. T., & Weisfeld, G. E. (2017). Sex and Infidelity. *The psychology of marriage: An evolutionary and cross-cultural view*, 251-64.

Dollahite, D. C., Marks, L. D., & Dalton, H. (2018). Why religion helps and harms families: A conceptual model of a system of dualities at the nexus of faith and family life. *Journal of Family Theory & Review*, *10*(1), 219-241.

Dollahite, D. C., & Lambert, N. M. (2007). Forsaking all others: How religious involvement promotes marital fidelity in Christian, Jewish, and Muslim couples. *Review of Religious Research*, 290-307.

Ellison, C. G., Henderson, A. K., Glenn, N. D., & Harkrider, K. E. (2011). Sanctification, stress, and marital quality. *Family Relations, 60*(4), 404-420.

Erickson, E. H. (1963). Childhood and society.

Farley, M. (2008). *Just Love: A framework for Christian sexual ethics.* Bloomsbury Publishing USA.

Fonagy, P. (1999). Points of contact and divergence between psychoanalytic and attachment theories: Is psychoanalytic theory truly different? *Psychoanalytic Inquiry, 19*(4), 448-480.

Fox, T. (1995). *Sexuality and Catholicism*. George Braziller.

Fromherz, F. & Sattler, S. (2023). *No Guilty Bystander: The extraordinary life of Bishop Thomas Gumbleton*. Orbis Books.

Garnets, L. D. (2002). Sexual orientations in perspective. *Cultural Diversity and Ethnic Minority Psychology*, *8*(2), 115.

Gottman, J. (2023). *What Predicts Divorce?: The relationship between marital processes and marital outcomes*. Routledge.

Gottman, J. M., & Krokoff, L. J. (1989). Marital interaction and satisfaction: a longitudinal view. *Journal of Consulting and Clinical Psychology*, *57*(1), 47.

Gudorf, C. (1994). *Body, Sex, and Pleasure: Reconstructing Christian sexual ethics*. Pilgrim Press.

Guindon, A. (1976). *The Sexual Language: An essay in moral theology*. University of Ottawa Press.

Guindon, A. (1986). *The Sexual Creators: An ethical proposal for concerned Christians*. University Press of America.

Haley, J. (1992). *Problem-solving therapy*. John Wiley & Sons.

Hall, J. A. (2015). Sexual selection and humor in courtship: A case for warmth and extroversion. *Evolutionary Psychology*, *13*(3), 1474704915598918.

Hamer, D. H., Hu, S., Magnuson, V. L., Hu, N., & Pattatucci, A. M. (1993). A linkage between DNA markers on the X chromosome and male sexual orientation. *Science*, *261*(5119), 321-327.

James, W. (1902). *The Varieties of Religious Experience. Gifford lects., 1901-1902*.

Jung, C. G. (1989). *Memories, Dreams, Reflections* (Vol. 268). Vintage.

Hazan, C., & Shaver, P. R. (1994). Attachment as an organizational framework for research on close relationships. *Psychological Inquiry*, *5*(1), 1-22.

Hines, M. (2011). Prenatal endocrine influences on sexual orientation and on sexually differentiated childhood behavior. *Frontiers in Neuroendocrinology*, *32*(2), 170-182.

Hooker, E. (1957). The adjustment of the male overt homosexual. *Journal of Projective Techniques*, *21*(1), 18-31.

Janssens, L. (1990). Personalism in moral theology. In Curran, C. (ed.), *Moral Theology: Challenges for the future* (pp. 94-107). Paulist Press.

Johnson, E. A. (2007). *Quest for the Living God: Mapping frontiers in the theology of God*. Bloomsbury Publishing.

Kaur, T., & Bhargava, M. (2016). Correlates of marital harmony. *Indian Journal of Health and Wellbeing*, *7*(9), 893.

Kearns, J. N., & Leonard, K. E. (2004). Social networks, structural interdependence, and marital quality over the transition to marriage: a prospective analysis. *Journal of Family Psychology*, *18*(2), 383.

King, B. M., & Regan, P. (2019). *Human Sexuality Today*, *9E*. Pearson.

Kosnik, A. et al (1977). *Human Sexuality: New directions in American Catholic thought*. Paulist Press.

Kosnik, A. R. (1975). Forming the Christian Catholic conscience. *Hospital Progress*, *56*(8), 51-54.

Kosnik, A.R. (1971) Penance and crisis in conscience. *Jurist*.

Labouvie-Vief, G. (1990). Modes of knowledge and the organization of development. *Adult Development*, *2*, 43-62.

Laing, R. (1959). *The Divided Self: An existential study in sanity and madness*. Tavistock Publications.

Lichter, D. T., & Carmalt, J. H. (2009). Religion and marital quality among low-income couples. *Social Science Research, 38*(1), 168-187.

Mahler, M. S. (2018). *The Psychological Birth of the Human Infant: Symbiosis and individuation*. Routledge.

Mahoney, A. (2010). Religion in families, 1999–2009: A relational spirituality framework. *Journal of Marriage and Family, 72*(4), 805-827.

Mahoney, A., & Cano, A. (2014). Introduction to the special section on religion and spirituality in family life: Delving into relational spirituality for couples. *Journal of Family Psychology, 28*(5), 583.

Mahoney, A., Pargament, K. I., & DeMaris, A. (2009). Couples viewing marriage and pregnancy through the lens of the sacred: A descriptive study. In *Research in the Social Scientific Study of Religion, Volume 20* (pp. 1-45). Brill.

Main, M. (1996). Introduction to the special section on attachment and psychopathology: 2. Overview of the field of attachment. *Journal of Consulting and Clinical Psychology, 64*(2), 237.

Maslow, A. (1970). *Motivation and Personality, 2E*. Harper & Row.

McCormick, R. (1977). Commentary on the *Declaration on Certain Questions Concerning Sexual Ethics*. In Curran, C. & McCormick R., (Eds.), *Readings in Moral Theology, No. 8: Dialogue about Catholic Sexual Teaching* (pp. 559-576).

McCormick, R. (1989). *Reflection on Moral Dilemmas Since Vatican II*. Georgetown University Press.

McNeill, J. (1976). *The Church and the Homosexual*. Sheed, Andrews, & McMeel, Inc.

Meyer-Bahlburg, H. F., Dolezal, C., Baker, S. W., & New, M. I. (2008). Sexual orientation in women with classical or non-classical congenital adrenal hyperplasia as a function of degree of prenatal androgen excess. *Archives of Sexual Behavior, 37*, 85-99.

Molz, M. (2002). *Polish and Proud: A Kosnik family history 1830 – 2002*. Author.

National Conference of Catholic Bishops (NCCB) (1992). *Program of Priestly Formation*. Author.

Oswald, R., Blume, L., Marks, S. (2004). Decentering heteronormativity: A model for family studies. In *Sourcebook of Family Theory and Research: An interactive approach*. Sage.

Pargament, K. I. (2001). *The Psychology of Religion and Coping: Theory, research, practice*. Guilford press.

Piechota, A., Ali, T., Tomlinson, J. M., & Monin, J. K. (2022). Social participation and marital satisfaction in mid to late life marriage. *Journal of Social and Personal Relationships, 39*(4), 1175-1188.

Riggle, E. D., Wickham, R. E., Rostosky, S. S., Rothblum, E. D., & Balsam, K. F. (2017). Impact of civil marriage recognition for long-term same-sex couples. *Sexuality Research and Social Policy, 14*, 223-232.

Rizzuto, A. M. (1979). *Birth of the Living God: A psychoanalytic study*. University of Chicago Press.

Rogers, C. R., (1961). *On Becoming a Person: A therapist's view of psychotherapy*. Houghton Mifflin.

Salway, T., Juwono, S., Klassen, B., Ferlatte, O., Ablona, A., Pruden, H., ... & Lachowsky, N. J. (2021). Experiences with sexual orientation and gender identity conversion therapy practices among sexual minority men in Canada, 2019–2020. *PloS one, 16*(6), e0252539.

Salzman, T. A., & Lawler, M. G. (2008). *The Sexual Person: Toward a renewed catholic anthropology*. Georgetown University Press.

Savin-Williams, R. C. (2006). Who's gay? Does it matter? *Current directions in psychological science, 15*(1), 40-44.

Selçuk, E., & İmamoğlu, O. (2018). Cultural and self-related considerations in relationship well-being: With particular reference to marriage in Turkey. In *Psychology of Marriage: An evolutionary and cross-cultural view*. Lexington Books.

Sieburg, E. (1985). *Family Communication: An integrated systems approach*. Gardner Press.

Sipe, A. R. (1995). *Sex, Priests, and Power: Anatomy of a crisis*. Psychology Press.

Spencer, A. T., Marks, L. D., Dollahite, D. C., & Kelley, H. H. (2021). Positive relational transformation in religious families: Supports and catalysts for meaningful change. *Family Relations, 70*(5), 1514-1528.

Stafford, L., David, P., & McPherson, S. (2014). Sanctity of marriage and marital quality. *Journal of Social and Personal Relationships, 31*(1), 54-70.

Stephenson, E., & DeLongis, A. (2019). A 20-year prospective study of marital separation and divorce in stepfamilies: Appraisals of family stress as predictors. *Journal of Social and Personal Relationships*, *36*(6), 1600-1618.

Streed Jr, C. G., Anderson, J. S., Babits, C., & Ferguson, M. A. (2019). Changing medical practice, not patients-putting an end to conversion therapy. *The New England Journal of Medicine*, *381*(6), 500-502.

Swidler, L., & Küng, H. (Eds.). (1987). *The Church in Anguish: Has the Vatican Betrayed Vatican II?* Harper & Row.

Swift-Gallant, A., Coome, L. A., Aitken, M., Monks, D. A., & VanderLaan, D. P. (2019). Evidence for distinct biodevelopmental influences on male sexual orientation. *Proceedings of the National Academy of Sciences*, *116*(26), 12787-12792.

Trispiotis, I., & Purshouse, C. (2022). 'Conversion therapy' as degrading treatment. *Oxford Journal of Legal Studies*, *42*(1), 104-132.

Watzlawick, P., Beavin, J., & Jackson, D. (1967). *Pragmatics of Human Communication: A study of interactional patterns, pathologies, and paradoxes.* Norton.

Weisfeld, G., Weisfeld, C., Dillon, L., (Eds.) (2018). *The Psychology of Marriage: An evolutionary and cross-cultural view.* Lexington Books.

Weisfeld, G. E. (2018). Humor in marriage. *The Psychology of Marriage: An evolutionary and cross-cultural view*, *237*.

Weisfeld, G. E., Weisfeld, C. C., & Goetz, S. M. (2017). Towards a model of marriage. *The Psychology of Marriage: An Evolutionary and Cross-Cultural View*, *317*.

Weisfeld, C. C., Silveri, A., & Fedon-Keyt, E. (2018). The American Families in the 21st Century. *The Psychology of Marriage: An Evolutionary and Cross-Cultural View*, 149.

Wilcox, W. B., & Dew, J. (2010). Is love a flimsy foundation? Soulmate versus institutional models of marriage. *Social Science Research*, *39*(5), 687-699.

Zhang, X., Li, J., Xie, F., Chen, X., Xu, W., & Hudson, N. W. (2022). The relationship between adult attachment and mental health: A meta-analysis. *Journal of Personality and Social Psychology*, *123*(5), 1089.

Acknowledgments

Tony Kosnik was viewed by many as "ahead of his time." It has been almost fifty years since the publication of *Human Sexuality*, and it continues to evoke strong reactions. I have long wanted to share Tony's story. To set the record straight. To remind the leadership of our Church of the importance of Tony's vision. Of the urgent need to move forward in the area of sexual ethics, as it has done with social justice.

This book is the result of a long process, which I have undertaken over the last six or seven years. The years of COVID, while dreadful and isolating, provided sustained time and focus for writing. I began by putting together chapter by chapter, sharing the "pieces" with my writing group, and slowly pulling it all together. This is not a project that I could have done alone. I have many people to thank for their help and support for my work.

First of all, I want to thank my publisher, David Crumm, and his Front Edge team, especially Susan Stitt and Dmitri Barvinok, for their endless support and hard work in getting my book to the finish line, as well as their patience in guiding me through the process of publication. A special thanks to Rodney Curtis for the wonderful photos!

Thank you to Carol and Bill Mitchell, who provided encouragement and support at the beginning of this process of sharing—what is for me a very personal journey. And a special thank you to Bill for all of his edits, for his willingness to read anything that I sent, for his quick turnaround, and for his persistence in getting me to a publisher.

Thank you to Bill Carroll, one of the co-writers of *Human Sexuality*, for his help in understanding some of the backstory of this work, including the collaborative process for writing undertaken by the co-authors. And for his encouragement at the beginning of my work on Tony's story. And thank you to Sister Agnes Cunningham, another co-author of *Human Sexuality*, for her kindness following Tony's death and her encouragement of my work on his story.

Thank you to all of the members of the Detroit Writers Group, especially John Gallagher, Anthony Ambrogio, Claire Crabtree, Nancy Shattuck, and the late Robin Watson, for their willingness to read all of the pieces of Tony's story, for their helpful edits, and for their encouragement as I worked to put the pieces together.

Thank you to my sister, Betsy, whose artwork graces the cover of *God in the House*, for her beautiful creative work. What a tribute to Tony! He would be so pleased to see this.

Thank you to Dr. Carol Weisfeld, my long-time partner in teaching Human Sexuality to the Clinical Ph.D. students at the University of Detroit Mercy, for her work on the Preface to this book. She has supported my academic writing over the years and has taught me much about marriage research.

Thank you to Dr. Bob Fink for his enthusiasm and willingness to read my work. He has provided valuable feedback from a social science perspective.

Thank you to Sister Jeannine Gramick, for her kind words about Tony, and for her work on the Afterword of this book. Her leadership of New Ways Ministry to LGBTQ Catholics, in the face of strong opposition by the Catholic hierarchy, continues to be inspirational.

And thank you to Charlie Curran, Tom Lumpkin, John Gallagher, Bill Mitchell, and Sue Sattler for their endorsements. For their careful reading of my manuscript and thoughtful comments. Charlie Curran and Tom Lumpkin have each reminded me that they are approaching the end of their journey. I am so grateful to have had the opportunity to share my work with them before they leave us.

I want to extend special thanks to the members of Re-Group, who have inspired me with their own stories of leaving religious life and the priesthood to begin new life, and who continue to provide me with support and understanding. Together with Rev. Paul Chateau, Marilyn Drader, Bobbie Williams, Sister Jean Gamache and her hospice team, they formed Tony's last group of traveling companions.

About the Author

Margaret "Peggy" Stack, Ph.D., ABPP is a licensed clinical psychologist who is also a Diplomate in Clinical Psychology from the American Board of Professional Psychology, based in southeast Michigan. She married the Rev. Dr. Anthony "Tony" Kosnik on May 25, 2002. They were together until his death on September 22, 2017. Peggy grew up in West Bloomfield, Michigan, and her family was part of Our Lady of Refuge parish, where she attended grade school. Our Lady of Refuge is located across the street from Sts. Cyril and Methodius Seminary where Tony studied and worked for thirty-eight years. Although there were visits to the seminary, and various priests from the seminary helped out with Sunday liturgy and sacraments, Peggy and Tony did not meet until much later. During their marriage, they belonged to Regroup—a support group for priests and religious who had left the priesthood and religious life and married; Elephants in the Living Room; and Catholics for the Common Good.

In 2012, they took on the role of helping to raise Peggy's two grandchildren.

Dr. Stack has maintained an outpatient mental health practice for four decades, providing services for children, adolescents, and adults, including individual and group psychotherapy, family and marital therapy, psychological evaluation, consultation, and workshops for various professional and community organizations. Her areas of specialization include trauma; marriage and family issues; services to clergy and religious, both treatment and evaluation of seminary applicants and candidates for the Permanent Diaconate and religious life; and forensic evaluations. She worked as a consultant to the Oakland County Circuit Court Family Division for twenty-three years, where she conducted psychological evaluations of adjudicated delinquents and individuals referred because of neglect and/or abuse, competency and criminal responsibility evaluations, provided expert witness services, and staff training. She previously served on an advisory board for cases of clergy abuse for the Archdiocese of Detroit.

Dr. Stack is retired from her position as Associate Professor of Psychology at the University of Detroit Mercy, where she spent twenty-three years. She taught at the graduate and undergraduate levels, courses in assessment, basic psychoanalytic concepts, human sexuality, religion and psychology, developmental psychology, and case conference. In addition to teaching, she held various administrative roles. She was Director of Clinical Training for the Clinical Ph.D. Program at UDM for a five-year term, and she was Director of the University Psychology Clinic (training clinic for the Ph.D. program) for a ten-year term. She has continued to provide clinical supervision for students in the Ph.D. program at UDM. Her primary areas of research interest have included LGBTQ issues, spirituality, and delinquent behavior in adolescents. She has presented and/or published papers on marital conflict, spirituality and religiosity in marriage, family systems, psychoanalytic theory, gender differences in married couples' nonverbal behavior, behavioral differences in happily married couples, constructing LGBTQ discourse in a Catholic context, attitudes toward sexual minorities at an urban Catholic university, sexual questions for Christian pastors, social competence in adjudicated adolescents, and risk factors contributing to adult recidivism of adjudicated delinquents.

Connect With Margaret Stack

Thank you for reading God in the House. If this book resonated with you, please help others discover it by leaving a review on Amazon or Goodreads.

Resources & Speaking

Visit www.GodInTheHouse.com for:

- Free discussion guide download
- Additional resources
- Author information

Margaret is available for interviews and speaking engagements at churches, community groups, and podcasts. Contact her at GodintheHouseBook@gmail.com.

Stay Connected

LinkedIn: linkedin.com/in/margaret-stack-0bab75307

Help spread the message of "God in the House" by sharing with friends, book clubs, and faith communities who would benefit from learning more about the Rev. Anthony Kosnik and his groundbreaking work.

National Catholic Reporter
Beacon of Justice, Community, and Hope
by Lawrence B. Guillot

Discover how the nonprofit National Catholic Reporter Publishing Company became the leader in independent journalism about the Catholic role in faith life, peace, justice, climate, and gender issues.

NATIONAL CATHOLIC REPORTER

BEACON of JUSTICE, COMMUNITY, and HOPE

HOW NCR HAS SUSTAINED INDEPENDENT JOURNALISM FROM VATICAN II TO POPE FRANCIS

Lawrence B. Guillot

FOREWORD BY THOMAS C. FOX

FRONT EDGE
PUBLISHING
YOUR IDEAS TAKE FLIGHT

https://www.ncronline.org/NCRbook

Hope For The City

by Jack Kresnak

This is the story of Father Bill Cunningham, Eleanor Josaitis, and others who were drawn to the mission of Focus Hope. It is a captivating retelling of an English teacher who wore a Roman collar, rode a Harley-Davidson, and marched with Dr. King across the Edmund Pettus bridge, a suburban mother of five who organized marriage enrichment events before she persuaded her husband to move into Detroit, and the 1967 riot that exposed systemic racial inequality and the civil rights organization that evolved.

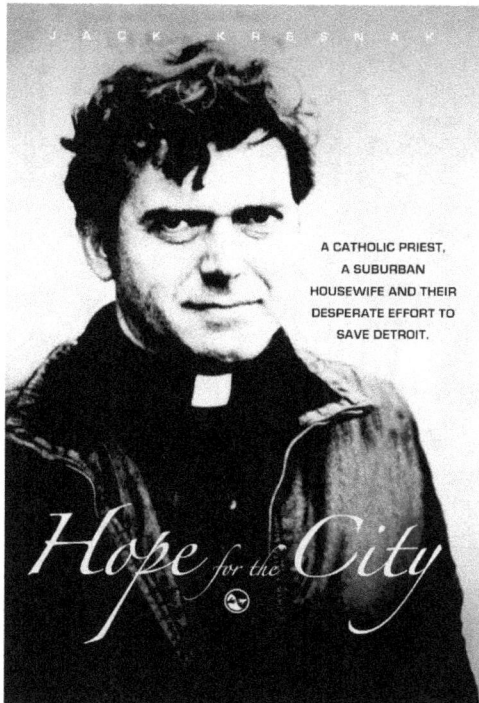

JACK KRESNAK

A CATHOLIC PRIEST,
A SUBURBAN
HOUSEWIFE AND THEIR
DESPERATE EFFORT TO
SAVE DETROIT.

Hope for the City

Cass Community Publishing House

https://ccpublishinghouse.org/

100 Questions & Answers About U.S. Catholic
by Michigan State University School of Journalism

Who are Catholics today? Discover the faith, practices and diversity behind the headlines with *100 Questions and Answers About U.S. Catholics*, a guide to understanding America's 70 million Catholics as well as Pope Francis' global influence.

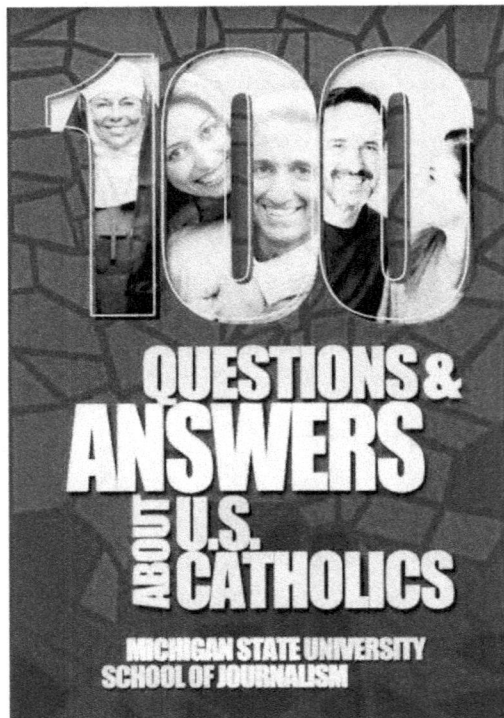

MSU Bias Busters

Friendship & Faith
by The Women of WISDOM

This is a book about making friends, which may be the most important thing you can do to make the world a better place and transform your own life in the process. Making a new friend often is tricky, as you'll discover in these dozens of real-life stories by women from a wide variety of religious and ethnic backgrounds.

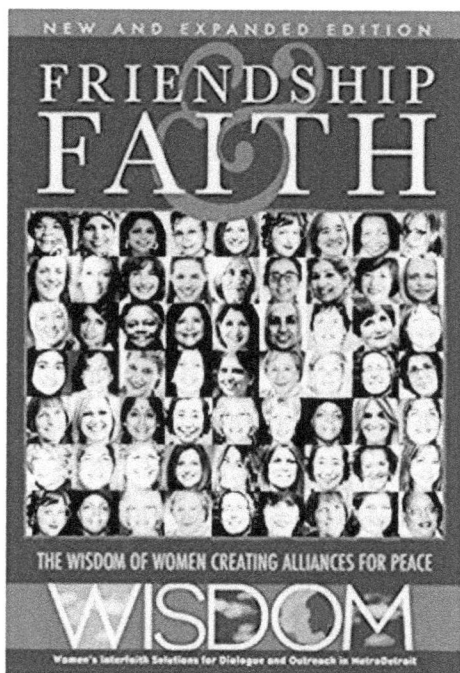

FRONT EDGE
PUBLISHING
YOUR IDEAS TAKE FLIGHT

https://www.interfaithwisdom.com/